Capitalism

Jürgen Kocka

Capitalism
A Short History

Translated by Jeremiah Riemer

PRINCETON UNIVERSITY PRESS

PRINCETON AND OXFORD

First published in Germany under *Geschichte des Kapitalismus*,
by Jürgen Kocka. © Verlag C. H. Beck oHG, München 2014

English translation copyright © 2016 by Princeton University Press

Published by Princeton University Press, 41 William Street,
Princeton, New Jersey 08540

In the United Kingdom: Princeton University Press, 6 Oxford Street,
Woodstock, Oxfordshire OX20 1TW

press.princeton.edu

Jacket art: *Top*, Amsterdam Stock Exchange around 1800, from the Museum of
American Finance. *Bottom*, New York Stock Exchange, early 20th century.
Courtesy of Shutterstock

ISBN 978-0-691-16522-6

Library of Congress Control Number: 2015955567

British Library Cataloging-in-Publication Data is available

This book has been composed in ITC Stone Serif Std

Printed on acid-free paper ∞

Printed in the United States of America

1 3 5 7 9 10 8 6 4 2

Contents

Preface to the English Edition

Capitalism is an essential concept for understanding modernity. By the same token, its history can serve as a key for explaining the most important socio-economic changes of the past. Debates about capitalism lead into discussions about the most pressing problems of the present time, ranging from globalization, the war against poverty, and climate change, through growing social inequality, to the prospects for progress and its human costs. At the same time, as a concept of historical synthesis capitalism is unsurpassed, bringing together the economic, social, cultural, and political dimensions of the past.

Capitalism is at once a tool of scholarly insight and of social critique. This dual function has made it suspicious to some but all the more interesting to others. Both functions could, but need not, stand in each other's way. Over the last several decades, the concept has made a forceful comeback in both public discussions and the social sciences.

But the concept remains controversial. It is still too frequently the ill-defined component of a one-sided narrative. It can be mythologized and distorted. Ardent simplifications abound among capitalism's critics and defenders alike.

This book offers a concise overview of the genesis and controversial development of the concept, and of the history of capitalism from antiquity to the present time. It distinguishes among different types of capitalism, especially among merchant capitalism, plantation capitalism, industrial capitalism, and finance capitalism. It discusses capitalism as an engine of innovation and growth, but also as a source of crisis, exploitation, and alienation. While the capitalist record of the West takes center stage, its global dimensions and expansion are carefully reconstructed, too. Central topics include "work in capitalism," "market and state," as well as "financialization." The book also deals with capitalism and its critique as a topic of intellectual history and of religious thought.

It is emphasized that capitalism has been highly transmutable over time, that it has flourished under very different social and political conditions, and that it can be shaped by politics and society. In this respect, the critique of capitalism has been and continues to be of outmost importance.

This introduction to the history of capitalism first appeared in German. For this edition it has been thoroughly revised, updated, and supplemented so as to make it more accessible and relevant for English-speaking readers.

Jürgen Kocka
Berlin, August 2015

Capitalism

1

$\textcircled{0}$

What Does Capitalism Mean?

The Emergence of a Controversial Concept

Capitalism is a controversial concept. Many scholars avoid it. To them it seems too polemical, since it emerged as a term of critique and was used that way for decades. The term is defined in different ways, and frequently not defined at all. It encompasses a great deal, and it is hard to delineate. Would it not be better to dispense with the concept and, say, talk about a "market economy"?

On the other hand, there is a long line of serious-minded scholars in the social sciences and cultural studies who have contributed a great deal of substance to the discussion about capitalism. A quarter century after the end of the Cold War, which was also a war of words in which key concepts were weapons, the term has returned to the scholarly discourse with a vengeance. The international financial and debt crisis that started in 2008 has added fuel to the fire of critical interest in capitalism. We are witnessing a new boom in course offerings about the history of capitalism on American college campuses, and the number of books and articles with "capitalism" in the title is on the rise. In Europe, too, the concept is now more newsworthy than it has been in a long while, even if its renewed topicality is more noticeable among journalists, social scientists, and cultural studies scholars than with economists.[1] But if the term is going to be used, one should be familiar with its history and define it sharply.

The term *capitalism* only gained acceptance in French, German, and English, after some sporadic antecedents, in the second half of the nineteenth century, although *capital* and *capitalist* had already become part of the vernacular in those languages. Let us take German as an example: there the concept of "capital" migrated from the language of merchants (where it was frequently used, at the latest, by the early sixteenth century) into the terminology of the social and economic sciences that were emerging in the seventeenth and eighteenth centuries. Initially the concept meant money (either invested or lent), and then later assets consisting of money, monetary values, commercial paper, commodities, and manufacturing plant, though always "in regard to the profit that it should yield" (1776), instead of being consumed or hoarded.

Since the seventeenth century, "capitalist" stood for the "capital-rich man who has cash monies and great wealth and can live from his interest and rents" (1756). More specifically, those designated as "capitalists" include merchants, bankers, pensioners, and other persons who lend money and thus "broker or deal in capital" (1717). In the meantime, "capitalist" also stood for all those engaged in the acquisition of wealth "if they accumulate the surplus of their labor, their earnings, over and above their required consumption, in order to use the surplus anew toward production and labor" (1813). Starting in the late eighteenth century, moreover, capitalists were increasingly viewed in contrast, and soon in outright opposition, to workers, and as the "class of wage masters (merchant-employers, factory entrepreneurs, and merchants)" who did not live off wages or rents but from profits (1808). Imbuing the concept with connotations of a class society, something already in evidence early in the nineteenth century, intensified in the ensuing decades as public poverty grew, revolutionary tensions erupted in 1848–1849, and industrialization with its factory system and wage labor also caught on in continental Europe, while observers, well into the early nineteenth century, drew their illustrative material above all from England, the country that had pioneered capitalist industrialization.[2]

Apart from a few early instances that did not really shape linguistic usage, the term *capitalism* initially reflected above all this imbuing of the term with criticism of the class society, a usage that happened just as the term started to catch on in the middle of the nineteenth century, originally in French, then also in German beginning in the 1860s, and somewhat later in England. In 1850 the socialist Louis Blanc criticized capitalism as the "the appropriation of capital by some to the exclusion of others." In 1851 Pierre Joseph Proudhon condemned land on the Parisian housing market as a "fortress of capitalism" while advocating measures against exorbitant rents and speculation. Then, in 1867, a representative French dictionary cited the term *capitalisme* as a neologism, used "power of capital or of capitalists" to describe it, and referred to Proudhon. In Germany in 1872, the socialist Wilhelm Liebknecht lashed out against the "moloch of capitalism" plying its dreadful trade on the "battlefields of industry."[3]

In German, at least, the term rapidly outgrew its original polemical thrust and became more widespread. Although Karl Marx rarely used the noun "capitalism," in the 1850s and 1860s he wrote profusely and effectively about the "capitalist mode of production." The conservative economist Johann Karl Rodbertus, who sympathized with state-socialist ideas, asserted in 1869 that "capitalism has become a social system." In 1870 Albert Schäffle, a liberal-conservative professor of political economy, published his book *Capitalism and Socialism with Special Attention to Forms of Business and Property*. In this book he delved into the conflict between wage labor and capital. He advocated state-sponsored reforms in order to mitigate those conflicts, and he defined capitalism as a national and international "organism" of production under the leadership of "entrepreneurial" capitalists competing for the highest profits. "The Socialists are correct," he added, "when they declare that the present economy is characterized by the capitalist mode of production," that is, by the hegemony of "capitalism." There is a reference to Schäffle in *Meyers Konversations-Lexikon* from 1876, when this German household encyclopedia treated "capitalism" for the first time, though in an entry on "capital." In 1896 this widely used reference work included a separate entry for "capitalism" with a differentiated argument about what the encyclopedia now described as a "designation for the capitalist production method, as opposed to the socialist or collectivist" one.

In 1902 Werner Sombart's great work *Modern Capitalism* was published, a book that contributed decisively to making the term part of the vernacular. Subsequent to this, there was a rapid expansion of the social science and historical literature that dealt with the theory, history, and present state of capitalism, to a great extent in debate with Sombart. Although Sombart viewed his book as a continuation and completion of Marx's work, in fact its emphasis on the role of entrepreneurs and enterprises, his concept of the "capitalist spirit," and his perspective reaching back into the Italian High Middle Ages went well beyond Marx.[4]

In Great Britain, as early as 1851, the concept was not entirely unknown. But starting in the 1880s, it was reluctantly introduced to a wider public, especially in Fabian circles. John A. Hobson published a book, *The Evolution of Modern Capitalism,* in which he focused on the rise of the factory system. The *Encyclopaedia Britannica* first mentioned the concept in its 1910–1911 edition (still only in its entry on "capital"). The encyclopaedia then carried an entire separate entry on the term in 1922, defining capitalism as "a system in which the means of production were owned by private proprietors" who employed managers and workers for production.[5]

The history of the concept in the United States paralleled that of Great Britain, though there is evidence that the term was known to radical working-class circles before journalists and scholars adopted it. Among American writers, Thorstein Veblen was one of the first to use it in his 1914 book *The Instinct of Workmanship and the State of Industrial Arts.* He followed European authors in stressing that capitalism was much older than industrialization, growing out of the handicraft system, trade, and finance from the fifteenth and sixteenth centuries. But he emphasized that "its highest development comes with the advanced stages of the machine technology and is manifestly conditioned by the latter."[6]

Individualized property rights; commodification on markets for goods, labor, land and capital; the price mechanism and competition; investment, capital, and profit; the distinction between power-holding proprietors and dependent propertyless wage workers; tensions between capital and labor; rising inequality; the factory system and industrialized production—these were, in varying combinations, major characteristics of the concept of capitalism as it emerged in the period leading up to World War I. The term was mostly used to denote an economic practice or an economic system, frequently with special attention to its social and cultural consequences.

All in all, then, one may summarize that the concept emerged out of a critical spirit and from a comparative perspective. Usually it was used in order to make observations about one's own era, which was conceived, in marked contrast to earlier conditions, as new and modern. Or it was used to confront what was then the present status quo with socialism, first as an envisaged idea and then as a movement whose first stirrings could be observed. Only in the light of a sometimes transfigured memory of a different past, or of a better future envisioned as a socialist alternative, did the concept of capitalism emerge, mostly in the context of a critical outlook on the present of that time. Yet at the same time the concept was employed in the service of scholarly analysis. This dual function of the term made it suspicious to some, but all the more interesting to others. Both functions could, but did not need to, stand in each other's way. This is still the case today.

Three Classics: Marx, Weber, and Schumpeter

In the late nineteenth and early twentieth centuries, numerous intellectuals, social scientists, and cultural studies scholars regarded capitalism as *the* decisive contemporary feature of their era. Numerous historians were then already using the term in order to investigate the history of capitalism in previous centuries when the term did not yet even exist.[7] Many authors contributed to the broadening of the concept of capitalism from a politically tendentious term into an analytically sophisticated systemic concept. The following pages explore somewhat more comprehensively three thinkers whose now classic statements have shaped the discussion and definition of "capitalism" to this day: Karl Marx, Max Weber, and Joseph A. Schumpeter.

Karl Marx rarely used the term *capitalism*, and then only marginally. But Marx wrote so extensively and penetratingly about the capitalist mode of production that his understanding of capitalism shaped following generations more strongly than the work of any other single person. The main components of the Marxist concept of capitalism may be summarized in four points.

1. Marx saw the *market*, which presumed a division of labor and money economy, as a central component of capitalism. He emphasized how a merciless, cross-border competition spurred

technological and organizational progress while
simultaneously positioning market players
against each other. He brought out the *compulsive
character* of the "law" of the market, a law capitalists and workers, producers and consumers, sellers
and buyers had to obey on penalty of failure, no
matter what their individual motives might be.

2. Marx discussed at length capitalism's essentially
   unlimited *accumulation* as one of its distinguishing features, that is, the formation and continuous increase of capital more or less as an end in
   itself, initially as "original accumulation" owing
   to transfers from other sectors (not without ex-
   propriation and not without force), then later as
   the reinvestment of profits, but ultimately derived from the value that labor created: capital as
   congealed labor.

3. Marx saw the core of the capitalist mode of production in the tension between capitalists as owners of the means of production, along with the
   entrepreneurs and managers dependent on these
   owners, on the one hand, and workers, contractually bound but otherwise freely employed in return for wages and salaries without ownership of
   the means of production, on the other. Both sides
   were bound to each other, by an exchange relationship (labor power or service against wages or
   salary, labor or labor power as commodity) and by
   a relationship of dominance and dependency that
   enabled the "exploitation" of workers by capitalists: exploitation in the sense that a portion of

value earned by workers, so-called surplus value, was not made available or paid out to them. This portion passed into the possession of the capitalist/entrepreneur, who used it partly to advance accumulation, partly to provide for what he consumed. The *capital–wage labor relationship* understood this way not only advanced the dynamism of the system. It simultaneously provoked class struggles that led over the long run to a confrontation between the *bourgeoisie and proletariat* facing each other as irreconcilable adversaries. This was, according to Marx, the precondition for revolution that, carried by the proletariat, will abolish the system of capitalism in favor of another, specifically socialist or communist, alternative, though Marx did not enter into any more detailed discussion of this alternative system. With this prediction, which could simultaneously be read as a call for the proletariat to attend to its historical mission, Marx transformed his theoretical conception into a practical political guideline, which is how many also understood it, starting in the late nineteenth century.

4. Marx described the enormous *dynamism of the capitalist system* that, sustained by the bourgeoisie, was dissolving everything traditional, was on its way to spreading out all over the world, and had not only the drive but also the capacity to extend its logic into noneconomic areas of life. Marx was convinced that the capitalist mode of production had a tendency to shape society,

culture, and politics decisively. What the economist Adam Smith had described as *commercial society* and the philosopher Georg Wilhelm Friedrich Hegel had called *bourgeois society*, Marx
portrayed as a social formation heavily influenced by the capitalist economy.

This picture of capitalism was critically influenced by
the dynamic conditions that Marx and Friedrich Engels
were able to observe in the second third of the twentieth
century in Germany and especially in western Europe.
Marx and Engels perceived the industrial revolution as an
epochal upheaval. They recognized the social dynamite
inherent in the burgeoning labor question. They concep-
tualized capitalism in a way that made it appear fully
formed only as *industrial capitalism*, with the factory and
wage labor at its core. Marx did not deny the existence of
older varieties of capitalism prior to industrialization, yet
they were not the subject of his investigations. He was
interested in capitalism in its modern, industrial form and
in its emergence—in England starting with the sixteenth
century.

Critiques of the Marxist conception are legion. With
good reason, he has been accused of having underesti-
mated the civilizing impact of markets while overestimat-
ing labor as the only source of newly created value. Marx
has also come in for criticism for his lack of attention to
the importance of knowledge and organization as sources
of productivity, his mistaken predictions about the social
repercussions of industrial capitalism, and his almost
quaintly old-fashioned European mistrust of the market,

exchange, and self-interest. Nevertheless, Marxist analysis remains an original, fascinating, and fundamental framework, a point of reference to this day for most subsequent interpreters of capitalism, no matter how much they may criticize Marx.[8]

Max Weber treated the subject of capitalism as part of a comprehensive history of occidental modernization. Against this background he removed the concept from its fixation on the industrial age. Unlike Marx, he did not expect capitalism to be destroyed by its own crises; rather, he feared the danger of petrification owing to an excess of organization and bureaucratization. He did not believe in the superiority of a future socialist system. His analysis was more wide ranging and reached further back into history than was the case with Marx.

For Weber, capitalist economic action was characterized by competition and exchange, orientation to market prices, the deployment of capital, and the search for profit. In his definition, capitalist economic action had to include a modicum of calculation, that is, weighing of expected risk, loss, and profit, as well as control over the profitability of the capital deployed. Weber was familiar with different forms of capitalism, such as the politically oriented capitalism and rentier capitalism of ancient Europe, or the "robber capitalism" that was associated since ancient times with wars and pillaging but has also not been absent from the speculation and exploitative businesses of modern finance capitalism. Above all, Weber was interested in *modern capitalism*, which was characterized by "formal, calculative rationality." He saw these features guaranteed above all by the structure of the capitalist *enterprise*. He emphasized how that enterprise was separated from the private household of economic agents, and he underlined the purposive rationality systematically built into the enterprise's organization of authority. The systematic purposive rationality of the capitalist enterprise included, in Weber's accounting, such elements as the division and coordination of labor, formally free labor by workers who do not own the means of production and are subjected to workplace discipline, that is, under the command and control of entrepreneurs and managers ultimately legitimated by ownership of capital. He elaborated on how effective management of a capitalist enterprise required, on the one hand, markets in money, credit, and capital. And, on the other hand, he regarded a specific kind of economic conviction as indispensable. In his judgment, this was not to be equated with unlimited acquisitive greed, but rather called for its "rational tempering," specifically in the form of a long-range and calculated readiness to invest and reinvest with the aim of long-term entrepreneurial success as such. An important source of this "spirit of capitalism" Weber saw in the Calvinist-Puritan ethic beginning in the sixteenth century (in contrast to Werner Sombart, who stressed the role of the Jews in establishing this attitude toward business since the Middle Ages).

Weber elaborated theoretically and historically on how capitalism in this sense presupposed a certain differentiation of social reality, which included a subsystem called *economy,* with relative autonomy, especially vis-à-vis politics: an autonomy that found concrete expression in freedom of contract and market-related entrepreneurship. On the other hand, he convincingly demonstrated how much the rise of capitalism across the centuries depended on extra-economic factors—especially on politics and law, on states, their wars, and their financial needs. And he was convinced that there was a huge "cultural significance" (*Kulturbedeutung*) to capitalism, which asserted its dynamism and its principles in many noneconomic areas of life as well. He emphasized that the kind of fully developed capitalism exhibiting all the features mentioned above was a phenomenon of the modern period. Weber was convinced that *modern capitalism* could only have emerged in the Occident, not least owing to the type of state formation that occurred here. He was no uncritical admirer of modern capitalism. While elaborating its "formal, calculative rationality," he nonetheless underscored that the growing economic efficiency this brought did not have to be accompanied by permanent growth in prosperity for every segment of the population. Rather, as Wolfgang Schluchter summarizes Weber's conviction, "capitalist economic action . . . does not provide for the satisfaction of needs but only for the satisfaction of 'needs with buying power.'" Here Weber saw a "fundamental and, in the last analysis, unavoidable element . . . of irrationality" at work.

Weber has also come in for a great deal of criticism. His thesis about the connection between the Puritan Protestant ethic and the spirit of capitalism has repeatedly been questioned empirically and strongly qualified (and this is even more true of Sombart's outmoded emphasis on the Jewish origins of the capitalist spirit). His assessment of whether non-Western civilizations, such as Islamic societies, were capable of capitalism, was not altogether free of prejudices, and it rested on a state of research that is obviously out of date after a century.[9] Yet his analyses are among the best that have ever been written about capitalism.

Joseph A. Schumpeter not only used the term *capitalism* in his own research, but he also deeply influenced the scholarly discussion with his book *Capitalism, Socialism and Democracy* (first published in 1942). Private property, the market mechanism, and an entrepreneurial economy were part of Schumpeter's definition of the word. "Capitalism is that form of private property economy in which innovations are carried out by means of borrowed money, which in general, though not by logical necessity, implies credit creation." By emphasizing the extension of credit and thereby the incursion of debt, Schumpeter makes a contribution that, after finance capitalism's disproportionate growth over the last several decades, is very topical today.

Schumpeter was especially concerned with explaining economic dynamics. He was searching for the mechanism by which the economy changed of its own accord. He found this in *innovation*, that is, the way that certain elements, resources, and opportunities combined to produce something economically new: new methods of production and distribution, new forms of organization in and also between businesses, the opening up of new markets for buying and selling goods, the production of new or significantly improved goods, the stimulation of new needs, and much more. It was clear to Schumpeter that introducing the new means replacing and sometimes destroying the old. In this context, he spoke of "creative destruction" as the core of capitalist development.

From this perspective, he developed his theory of the business cycle. For, in his view, innovations can trigger growth. They can cause waves of economic expansion in which innovative entrepreneurs are soon joined by many others following their lead before the wave loses its impetus, runs out of steam, and turns into a downswing until a new bundle of innovations leads to the start of a new cycle. This is the source of Schumpeter's keen interest in entrepreneurs, whom he saw as the carriers of those mechanisms of change he was investigating.

This is also the source of Schumpeter's conviction that credit is so important. For nobody can ever be completely certain about the success of innovations, and that success will only be assured, if ever, in the future. For this reason, and also because the returns innovations bring are only registered (if at all) at some later time, during the cycle's upswing, the entrepreneur carrying out innovations requires capital in advance, which he contracts as debt in order to pay it back with interest later if the project is successful. This connection between credit and the carrying out of innovations was recognized by Schumpeter as a specific feature and foundation of capitalism's dynamic force.[10]

He was convinced that capitalism had brought to not just a small minority but the broad majority of the population a degree of material well-being and personal freedom that was unique in human history. He also offered a psychological and sociological explanation for this enormous productivity and efficiency of the capitalist economy: this type of economy succeeds partly by awakening and partly by enlisting ever new motifs—such as the often illusory hope for enrichment and the all too justified fear of becoming déclassé—and seeing to it that extremely capable, ambitious, and energetic people are recruited and retained in leadership positions. But in spite of such impressive accomplishments, Schumpeter predicted the decline of capitalism. By expanding its principles into other spheres of life, capitalism would damage the very social preconditions that made it possible. Schumpeter illustrated this with such examples as the social institution of the extended family, which for a long time had been a source of motivation and energy for capitalist entrepreneurs but was increasingly being undermined by forces of instrumental rationality and individualism conducive to the capitalist spirit. Capitalism would fail owing to the unintended consequences of its own success.[11]

Schumpeter's work has come in for criticism. His prognosis was not confirmed in the second half of the twentieth century. His conception of innovation was too narrowly fixated on individual persons and major disruptive acts. His notion of fifty- to sixty-year business-cycle waves (*Kondratieffs*) remains highly controversial. His option for using the term *capitalism* was not emulated in mainstream economics, where society, politics, and culture were less and less included within its scope. But Schumpeter's work lives on among his followers and opponents. It is irreplaceable for the history of capitalism.

Other Voices and a Working Definition

There were many other thinkers who helped sharpen the concept. In the 1920 and 1930s, John Maynard Keynes saw the essence of capitalism in its appeal to the "money-making and money loving instincts of individuals as the main motive force of the economic machine." Moods, emotions, and accidents played a major role in capitalism, in his assessment, not just instrumental rationality and calculability, which were emphasized so strongly by Max Weber. Keynes saw "animal spirits" at work, forces he did not merely observe with disconcerted detachment. Rather, he acknowledged them as important driving forces behind the capitalist way of doing business, which he was convinced takes place under the pressure of incalculable uncertainty and needs these kinds of explosive charges. This assessment of Keynes—an astute, top-flight economist of his time well acquainted with business life—points to the gaps in capitalism's instrumental rationality that have to be filled by emotions. The critique of finance capitalism, particularly since its most recent crisis, which came to a head in 2008, picks up on Keynes's emphasis on animal spirits.[12]

Karl Polanyi's book *The Great Transformation*, first published in 1944, hardly used the term *capitalism*. Yet, focusing on English cases from the nineteenth century, it dealt with the formation of a market economy that was breaking away from its political and social moorings—its "embeddedness"—and tending toward self-regulation. The dynamic of this market economy, according to Polanyi, stood in sharp contrast to society's need for integration. According to him, the market had become a largely autonomous subsystem that forced permanent change, tore apart the social fabric, and prevented the emergence of a reliable social order with stable identities so long as legislation and public administration did not succeed in creating new forms of "embeddedness" and thereby curbing the market's destructive dynamism. Polanyi's book, which rests on a weak empirical foundation and is not compatible with the current state of research in economic history, misconstrues social history *before* capitalist industrialization, which was already much more strongly defined by markets and much less idyllic than Polanyi supposes. Conversely, the unleashing of market forces in the nineteenth and early twentieth centuries is strongly exaggerated. Yet conceptually the book does have important food for thought. In recent years it has exerted considerable influence on the critical analysis of capitalism in the social sciences.[13]

Most authors conceive of the market as a necessary but not sufficient criterion of "capitalism." The comparison frequently made during the decades of the Cold War between capitalism and the centrally administered economy of state socialism lent even greater prominence to the market as an essential component of capitalism. The historian Fernand Braudel wrote against this view. In his three-volume *Civilization and Capitalism, 15th–18th Century*, first published in France in 1979, he delivered penetrating descriptions of emerging capitalism while distinguishing it from the "market economy." In the latter category he includes local markets and business transactions by traders and most merchants, but also trade fairs and stock exchanges. By contrast, he confines the term *capitalism* to the business transactions of a small and quite exclusive upper echelon of rich, powerful capitalists who, depending on how matters stood in long-distance trade, were successful merchants, shipowners, insurers, bankers, and entrepreneurs but also landowning squires, and usually several of these simultaneously. In these upper echelons—which Braudel identified with capitalism, at least for the early modern period—market competition did not play a major role, while monopolization of market opportunities, usually facilitated by the closest of ties to the politically powerful, was all the more important.

In this way, Braudel was correctly drawing attention to how, over long periods of time, the interpenetration of market power and political power was much more the rule than was their tidy separation. Moreover, he trenchantly got to the heart of the way that oligopolistic and monopolistic tendencies can easily turn up in capitalism. These tendencies can work against the principle of competition that is supposed to be a fundamental characteristic of the market economy, and they can partially override it. Nonetheless, Braudel's definitional opposition of capitalism and market economy is misleading. Even in the early modern era, and even in its "upper echelon," the kind of capitalism taking shape was characterized by a great deal of competition, profit and loss, rise and fall, opportunity and risk. It was rooted in the market economy and, as a rule, contributed not to the elimination of markets but to their becoming more universal. Essentially, this remains true to this day.[14]

Immanuel Wallerstein and Giovanni Arrighi, among others, have taken up Braudel's concept of capitalism and his pathbreaking excursions into the extra-European history of capitalism. Their work has given impetus to the important question of capitalism's transnational and ultimately global dimensions. The *Communist Manifesto* had already predicted the global expansion of capitalism. In particular, socialist theorists of imperialism like Rudolf Hilferding, Rosa Luxemburg, and Lenin[15] had discussed the cross-border effects and interconnections of capitalism, especially the capitalist impulses behind imperialist expansion and dependencies between exploited peripheries and imperially dominant metropoles, as well as the link between capitalism and international conflicts. Various *dependencia* theories and, above all, Wallerstein's world-system approach developed these intellectual traditions in the third quarter of the twentieth century. And Arrighi advanced the globalization of research on capitalism by exploring the spatial shift of the world economy's center of gravity—from northern Italy in the late Middle Ages, via the Netherlands in the early modern era, and England since the eighteenth century, to the USA (twentieth century) and, perhaps, soon to China.[16] With the growing receptiveness of historical scholarship to global history that has taken place over the last two decades, capitalism is increasingly discussed as a phenomenon of global history.[17] This draws attention to the spatial component of capitalism, to capitalist expansion and trans-regional interconnections. New questions are being put on the agenda, and old ones are being reformulated, such as the question of the West's place in the history of capitalism. As a result, the definitions of *capitalism* that have largely been coined in Europe and North America could be subject to change over the long run. But this much is also clear: however much the concept and theories of capitalism are, by way of origin, products of Western experience and scholarship, just as little is their claim to validity and analytical power confined to the West.[18] Rather, these definitions constitute an invitation to historical inquiry that is transnational and global.

With these findings in the history of concepts and theories as a foundation, and after having examined additional proposals for defining the term,[19] I propose a working definition of *capitalism* that emphasizes decentralization, commodification, and accumulation as basic characteristics. First, it is essential that individual and collective actors have rights, usually property rights, that enable them to make economic decisions in a relatively autonomous and decentralized way. Second, markets serve as the main mechanisms of allocation and coordination; commodification permeates capitalism in many ways, including labor. Third, capital is central, which means utilizing resources for present investment in expectation of future higher gains, accepting credit in addition to savings and earnings as sources of investment funds, dealing with uncertainty and risk, and maintaining profit and accumulation as goals. Change, growth, and expansion are inscribed.[20]

I shall refrain from adding the existence of a business undertaking or enterprise as an additional feature of capitalism in order not to exclude less formalized variants by definition, variants that have been widespread across the centuries and are still—and again—so today. But there is a strong tendency to form business enterprises as capitalist units of decision-making, action, and accountability. When the enterprises are formed, their claim to accomplishment rests on "private" (meaning nongovernmental, noncommunal, noncollective) rights of property and use. They have some independence vis-à-vis the state and other social institutions, but also vis-à-vis the households of economic actors. On the inside, enterprises are primarily hierarchical in structure. The enterprise is an important space in which capital and labor enter into a relationship with each other: there is an interaction between capitalistically legitimated entrepreneurs employing a workforce, on the one hand, and the dependently employed, namely workers and salaried employees who do not own capital or the means of production, on the other hand. Workers are typically employed as wage workers on a contractual basis—that is, for a time, without involving their entire personality—and in this sense are free. Relations between capital and labor, between employers and employees, are an exchange relationship according to market principles on the one hand, and on the other hand an asymmetrical authority relationship that permits the absorption of "surplus value" and has a variety of consequences for society.[21]

This definition allows us to include in the investigation those manifestations of capitalism that merely represent minority phenomena within noncapitalist environments. However, in order to speak of a full-fledged "capitalist economy" or a "capitalist system," capitalist principles do need to have a certain dominance. This means not only dominance as a regulatory mechanism inside the economy (although this is also important) but also the tendency of capitalist principles to extend beyond the economy into other spheres of society and influence them to a greater or lesser extent. This dominance and pervasive influence of capitalist principles beyond the economic sphere has been the case no matter how much the anchoring of capitalism in noncapitalist relations has historically been the rule. The

system-extending character of capitalism reaching out beyond the economic sphere is capable of expressing itself to
very different degrees and in quite different forms. Capitalism is possible in different societies, cultures, and state for-
mations. At the same time, its outreach into noneconomic
areas of life certainly does have its limits, which are historically variable and can become influenced by politics.

Such a working definition delineates capitalism as an
ideal type, a model, that one uses even though one knows
that it is not wholly identical with historical reality. Instead, reality corresponds to it in ways and to degrees that
are different and ever changing. In this manner it is possible to apply the concept to eras going back a long way, eras
in which the concept was not yet in use and when what it
meant existed only in tiny rudiments, as trace elements
of a kind of proto-capitalism in small amounts , or only on
little capitalist islands in a sea of noncapitalist conditions.
As an ideal type, the concept could also be used to explore
realities that are still capitalistically structured but less so
than before. Perhaps there actually will be such realities of
declining degrees of capitalism in the future.

The following account cannot possibly aim at an exhaustive treatment of all countries and regions in which
capitalism has happened. Instead, it understands capitalism as a worldwide phenomenon whose most important
phases and variations, impulses, problems, and consequences it will unfold in chronological order and exem-
plify in different countries or regions. To that end, influential leading regions will be picked for each respective
phase and variant. For the early centuries of merchant
capitalism, I look at China, Arabia, and parts of Europe. In

the breakthrough phase of around 1500 to around 1800, when "modern capitalism" in Marx's and Weber's sense of the term emerged, western Europe moves into the center of the account, though with attention to European capitalism's global linkages. In the nineteenth and twentieth centuries, attention shifts to industrial capitalism and finally to the rise of finance capitalism, which will primarily be illustrated with European, North American, and some Japanese examples. Capitalism's accelerated globalization in the second half of the twentieth century and at the beginning of the twenty-first requires a look beyond the West, especially as it is experienced in East Asia. Overall, developments in Europe, and then in North America, take up the most space. This is justified by the subject: capitalism was a Western phenomenon for long stretches of its history, even if it would either not have developed or have developed differently without its global links. But the author's preferences undoubtedly also play a role here, since I am more at home in the history of the West than in that of other continents. Fully incorporating those other regions of the globe would have to be the aim of a more comprehensive account.

2

Merchant Capitalism

In the scholarly literature, there are different answers to the question of when capitalism began. The diversity of voices results from using different concepts of capitalism as well as from the fact that unambiguous turning points rarely occur in social and economic reality.[1] Early rudiments are easiest to find in long-distance trade. In Mesopotamia and the eastern Mediterranean, on the "Silk Road" and the great East-West trade route through the Indian Ocean, this trade was largely in the hands of independent merchants. These merchants traded on their own accounts, even if this was usually done in close coordination with the politically powerful, and often, moreover, in close cooperation with other merchants, typically in cross-border networks based on common ties of ethnicity, homeland, or religion. There was no lack of profit seeking, daring, dynamism, or a willingness to cope with insecurity and competition.

The first agglomerations of merchant capitalism may be observed in the intermittently emerging empires that developed serious cash requirements for their military undertakings and hence favored above all developing markets that promoted monetization and attempted to strengthen economic performance, also by building transport routes, operating mines (precious metals!), and securing a minimum of order. Early on, market and state formation went hand in hand.[2] For example, the civil service state of the Chinese Han dynasty (206 BCE–CE 220) made an effort to standardize the currency, expand market relations, and promote a lively long-distance trade carried out by independent merchants. At the same time, it intervened directly in trade and commerce. In the Roman imperial era (1 BCE–CE 5), the monetization of the economy and commercialization of everyday life in the big cities reached a high level, long-distance trade in foodstuffs and luxury goods flourished, the large latifundia produced for the market at a profit, and economic transactions like the sale or lease of land took place on a contractual basis aided by precise calculations. There was also no lack of more or less free wage workers. Yet on the whole the subsistence economy was predominant, slave labor was widespread, and "the strong drive to acquire wealth was not translated into a drive to create capital" (Moses Finley). The orientation toward secure rents was more widespread than the drive for profit. Productivity growth and macroeconomic growth were kept within limits, and the orientation toward war and booty was still stronger than the orientation toward long-term market success. This is why one sometimes hesitates to call the economy of Greco-Roman antiquity capitalist.[3]

China and Arabia

In order to examine what was going on with capitalism or its rudiments during the centuries that are summarized as the "Middle Ages" in European history, we turn our attention to three regions known for having been scenes of relevant developments in this period of time: China, the Indian Ocean region that increasingly came under Arab influence, and western Europe.

The basic pattern that emerged in China during the Han dynasty continued in the centuries to follow. It facilitated the expansion of international trade relations and an ever livelier exchange with regions to its west, that is, with India and the Arab world in particular. The Confucianism practiced by the civil servants who exercised political power included such elements as a rejection of pronounced inequality and hence of too much independent wealth, the promotion of agriculture, and state controls over money, the credit system, and trade. These controls extended as far as a willingness to operate estates, supply depots, and workshops under state management. Buddhism, which started in India and spread out from there to places in Asia where it was practiced above all by traders and merchants, had a more positive attitude toward commercial activity. Buddhist cloisters not only accepted extensive donations from believers. Eyed suspiciously by the state bureaucracy and at times suppressed, they also operated as centers of capital formation, lending, and of profit-making investment of capital in agricultural and commercial companies. In the middle of the eighth century, Guangzhou was depicted as a lively and prosperous port and mercantile city. Foreign visitors testified to the country's high living standard.

That living standard was especially true of China under the rule of the trade-friendly Sung dynasty (960–1279).

With the support of the government and its gigantic new fleet, the merchants expanded maritime trade, especially with Southeast Asia, India, the Arab world, East Africa, and even with Egypt. Domestically, too, the importance of money and market relations increased considerably. Through the thirteenth century in some regions, especially in the southeastern part of the country, the traditional subsistence economy developed into a different kind of economy, one relying on supraregional exports and producing both luxury goods and a variety of commercial consumer goods made out of stone, porcelain, and metal. In exchange, the region imported foodstuffs, especially rice, from other provinces. Overall, trade and industry spread in China, partly in workshops operated by civil servants or merchants where wage workers were continuously employed. The country exported above all processed products (porcelain, paper, silk, art objects, metalwares), but also tea and metals like tin and lead. It imported horses, spices, medicines, precious stones, and other luxury goods, but also cotton fabrics. To some extent, economic activities were subordinated to the central state, which also saw to it that streets and canals were built; intermittently exercised monopoly rights with respect to salt, tea, and incense; controlled the currency; and made an effort to control the business in bills of exchange, developed by merchant bankers since the ninth century but still quite elementary, that had led to the circulation of notes and represented a kind of de facto money. But in principle the economic boom was supported by profit-oriented merchants whose investments, although restricted by the state, were considerable, and whose social status rose in that period. Historians have discussed a Chinese "commercial revolution" in the eleventh and twelfth century. There were also pathbreaking technological innovations: gunpowder, the compass, and the printing press. In actuality, the boom happened in a mixed-economy system.

Much of this was continued when China was ruled by the invading Mongols (1279–1368) and then later by the Ming dynasty (1368–1644). But in the following centuries, China did not keep up the extraordinary dynamism that it had achieved under the Sung dynasty. This became most evident after Chinese policy shifted following the spectacular sea expeditions that Admiral Zheng-He, using large crews, successfully undertook to the distant coasts of western Asia and Africa on diplomatic missions for the emperor. In the 1430s policy shifted away from sea trade and opted for letting the fleet deteriorate, making foreign journeys more difficult for merchants and turning China inward. This much-discussed change of course, with its long-term impact, certainly coincided with the demanding task of protecting the empire's north against the Mongols and other possible invaders. It was the outcome of an internal power shift—within the tension-filled mixture of cooperation and conflict between state power and market economy, between merchants as junior partners and civil servants as senior partners—whereby a more conservative faction of landowners and Confucian civil servants emerged victorious. The ever-present mistrust of commerce and capital accumulation gained the upper hand. The Chinese form of merchant capitalism, politically controlled and embedded, proved poorly equipped to resist and insufficiently robust to oppose this political change of course by a powerful central state.[4]

A second major region for medieval merchant capitalism was located in the Arabian empire that existed under the Umayyads and Abbasids between the late seventh and mid-thirteenth centuries, encompassing western Asia, North Africa, and the Iberian peninsula, and established Islam as a world religion. Even as early as the emergence of Islam at the beginning of the seventh century, there was no lack of merchant capitalist elements. Mecca and Medina were then lively merchant cities conveniently located on major caravan routes. Mohammed himself came from an urban mercantile milieu. The spread of Islam, which went hand in hand with the construction of an Arab-dominated, Muslim-influenced state, soon to be an empire, happened unusually rapidly. This did not take place, however, primarily by way of merchants and the expansionary forces of the market but rather by political force, violence, and conquest—and with the enormous impetus of a newly created missionary religion that pursued universal aspirations and used highly efficient mercenary troops who quickly triumphed after the downfall of the Roman and Middle Eastern empires, subjugated various peoples, plundered in grand style, and complemented all this with a steady stream of slaves, mostly from the stock of its defeated enemies. In just a few years (until 632), the Arabian peninsula was subjugated, within two additional decades the Near and Middle East as well as Egypt and Libya were occupied, and in the late seventh and early eighth centuries there followed the incorporation of northwestern India, western North Africa, and the Iberian peninsula.

It was on the basis of this empire in formation, starting in the eighth century, that Arab and Persian merchants and traders, shipowners and seafarers, caravan operators and agents of all kinds began to dominate existing trade routes running through the Eurasian continent and the great maritime trading routes as they simultaneously developed new trade links: toward Africa, toward Southeast Asia, and into western Europe. The most important one was still the great East-West link from the Mediterranean across the Arabian deserts, Persian Gulf, and Indian Ocean toward India, Southeast Asia, and China. In the major harbors where silk and porcelain, gold and silver and all kinds of metals, but also linens and metal utensils, high-grade wood, spices and oils, furniture and jewelry, slaves, and many other goods were transshipped, stacked, sold and resold, the facilities that these transactions required were in the hands of Persians and Arabs who increasingly put together the ships' crews, led the caravans, and provided all the necessary information. Muslim-oriented law apparently provided a good foundation for concluding commercial-mercantile contracts, for borrowing, and for collecting debts. It provided viable cross-border rules, without which long-distance trade, risky in any event, could quickly deteriorate. On the basis of a common language, religion, and also to some extent culture, there emerged new networks of Arab merchants in which—in spite of all the conflicts, competition, and infractions of rules—it was possible to fall back on a potential of trust that reduced insecurity, facilitated cooperation, and so created market relationships across great distances and heterogeneous regions.

Yet the rise of long-distance trade also had a domestic impact. Prosperity was clustered along the trade routes. To be sure, the subsistence economy remained dominant everywhere in this expanse, as did the practice of skimming off acquired assets by exerting political authority rather than by recourse to the market. But the integration of many sites and regions in developing market relations did lead to a differentiation of agricultural and commercial products. Thus, one can show on the basis of examples from northeastern Persia between the seventh and eleventh centuries that some places specialized in damask or satin, others by contrast on processing pelts and hides. There were places there that concentrated on making soap and perfume, others on weapons, metal crockery, and tools. The workshops, which were involved in fluctuating price trends, also employed wage workers. Fruits, cane sugar, spices, and dried fish were among the products that specialized peasants ventured bringing to supra-local markets. In this way, the relationship between landowners, leaseholders, and slaves or workers was indirectly shaped by changing market relations. For all this business to take place, the assistance of traders and merchants was required, even if these dealers did not, as a rule, intervene in the organization of production.[5] The capital of the merchants derived *in part* from the large fortunes that grew out of earlier conquests and raids: an example of the kind of violent "original accumulation" that not infrequently stood at the cradle of capitalism. Family relationships might open access to resources from land-owning elites. Business partnerships were frequent, and they were used to finance and share in the risks of major undertakings, though usually only for a limited period (e.g., one or two years) until the enterprise in question, for example a major buying and selling expedition by ship, came to an end. There were legal requirements for these ventures, including stipulations for shareholding forms that were later designated in Europe by the term "Commenda." *In part*, the necessary capital came out of reinvested profits that had previously been made through trade. *Finally*, there was also borrowing on credit.

In these Islamic-influenced societies, the possibility of lending money at profit as a way of letting one's capital go to work, to "make it fruitful," was frequently used—this notion did exist there. The ban on interest anchored in the Koran—as well as in the Old Testament and the Talmud—could be skirted. On the one hand, the ban did not apply to "strangers": For this reason, Jews and Christians were predestined for the money and credit trade in the early Islamic world (as were Jews and Arabs, later, in the Christian Occident). On the other hand, going back to the early ninth century, there was a special advice-dispensing literature publicly explaining various tricks that could be used to get around the ban on interest. In Arabia, advanced credit instruments were developed, while checks and bills of exchange came into use even before the turn of the millennium. Checks could also be transferred across great distances, even if they could not yet be properly traded. These were techniques that in Europe would not be used before the twelfth and thirteenth century.[6] From the outset, Islam adopted a positive attitude toward trade. Hardly an Islamic thinker seems to have rejected the pursuit of profit as such as immoral or harmful to faith. Even the critique of wealth typical of early Christianity was missing. Influential Muslim scholars from the eleventh and twelfth century, such as the Persians Ghazali and al-Tusi, viewed the market not primarily as a site of competition or combat but as a place for cooperation and the expansion of mutual assistance via the division of labor and exchange, a little like the way Adam Smith would view these in the eighteenth century. State intervention into price setting was denied legitimacy, and in this regard the example of the Prophet was invoked. In unadorned language and without criticism, the fourteenth-century Arab historian Ibn Khaldun asserted that the business of commerce was "to make a profit by increasing capital, through buying goods at a low price and selling them at a high price, whether these goods consist of slaves, grain, animals, weapons, or clothing material." In the eleventh century, the literature mapped out the skills possessed by different types of merchants: these included the ability to predict future price developments, knowledge of currency and price relations in other countries, and access to reliable middlemen and warehouses in order to find and anticipate favorable sales conditions. The merchant enjoyed social recognition; like Sinbad the Sailor, he even had enough of the right stuff to become the fictional hero of folklore storytellers. In the last two centuries of the first millennium, the rudiments of a merchant capitalist bourgeoisie emerged in some parts of Arabia, more clearly here than anywhere else in the world at that time. Yet the merchant capitalists had no share in the political power exercised by the traditional elites, noble landowners, and military leaders. The bourgeoisie that was emerging here in a sporadic and rudimentary fashion was not a ruling class. Arab merchants were more removed from the state than their Chinese—and European—counterparts.[7]

Europe: Dynamic Latecomer

In the comparative perspective of global history, merchant capitalism developed relatively late in medieval Europe, but then differently than in Asia. With the political collapse of the Western Roman Empire in the fifth century, and in the midst of the instability of the Germanic tribes' migration period, economic life disintegrated, and capitalistic practices that had emerged in antiquity collapsed: this was again an example of the close connection, in this case negative, between the formation of states and markets. In the parts of Europe that had been ruled and influenced by the Roman Empire (excluding the eastern Mediterranean region, which continued to be part of the Byzantine or Eastern Roman Empire), there was a retrogression of the market economy, demonetization, and reversion to agriculture. Trade relations that had once extended from the Baltic Sea to China fell apart, cities and trading centers atrophied, and highways were deserted. On the whole, the household economy and self-sufficiency predominated, even if such institutions as monasteries often produced more than they consumed, attempted to sell the surplus at a profit, accumulated capital, and advanced money without interest, though not without gainful collateral. Trade was locally restricted, by and large, although coastal sea trade was never completely broken off, and Roman traditions did survive along the Mediterranean.

In medieval Europe, too, capitalistic practices caught on in long-distance trade. Between the twelfth and fifteenth centuries, trade between Europe and Asia that had heretofore been rather sporadic extended, with increasing density and regularity, from the coastal cities of northern Italy, southern France, and Catalonia to Egypt, Palestine, Syria, and Byzantium, and from there further eastward.[8] The Crusades of the twelfth century, which to some extent were raids, simultaneously upset and powerfully stimulated East-West trade. For a long time, this trade was managed by shipowners, merchants, and ship captains from Venice, Genoa, and somewhat later Florence, together with Pisa and Livorno, soon also points of departure for ships sent through the Straits of Gibraltar to France, Flanders, and England. Another important trade route ran through the seas in the north and linked Russia, Poland, and Scandinavia with Flanders, Brabant, and England. Yet routinely used and increasingly upgraded trade routes were also developed on land: these included the Alpine passages from Italy to southern Germany and further north, continuing along the Rhine route that led from Basle to the Netherlands, where there was an oversea connection to England; there were also links that emerged between these trade regions because of regular visits to trade fairs starting in the middle of the twelfth century (initially in the Champagne region of France).

Not only were the merchants who carried on this long-distance trade following capitalist principles, they were

also developing cooperative solutions in an effort to re-
duce the considerable risks associated with long journeys
over great distances. For the overland journey they banded
together into caravans, and they sent their ships out in
fleets, not infrequently numbering fifty to a hundred, well
armed in order to protect themselves against raids by rob-
bers and pirates (and sometimes also by competitors!). In
a time of weak states and widespread mistrust toward for-
eigners, traveling merchants from the same regional or
ethnic background who found themselves in the same distant destination often stayed in close contact with each
other, and even lived there together on a mostly temporary basis, separated from the native population, in trading stations, lodges, overseas branch offices, or specialized
urban districts, often with separate self-governing institutions and special legal jurisdictions of their own; these arrangements rested on a foundation of privileges the merchants had acquired from the relevant local authority in
exchange for services rendered. As a rule these were temporary associations among highly mobile persons, yet
they could also develop into long-term unions, the best-
known example of which is the Hanseatic League.[9]

Initially a union of traveling merchants with a common
background from certain (mostly northern German) cities, and *simultaneously* a powerful if loosely structured alliance of what was occasionally more than fifty cities, the
"German Hanse" defined shipping, trade, and politics in
the North and Baltic Sea region from the thirteenth to the
sixteenth centuries. There was trade in luxury goods like
spices and amber, but also with mass goods for daily use

by a wide range of buyers, goods that included wool, cloth, pelts and hides, fish, salt and grain, wooden and metal articles. Port cities like Lübeck, Hamburg, Stettin, Danzig, Bremen, Wismar, and Rostock were the leading places, but inland cities like Cologne, Magdeburg, and Braunschweig also belonged to the League. The Hanse League, moreover, had outposts (so-called *Kontoren*—branch offices or counting houses—in old commercial German) in such diverse places as Novgorod, Bergen, London, and Bruges.

The merchants of the Hanse liked to combine in pairs and form small trading companies that would last for several years. They shared what were frequently high profits: in the fourteenth and fifteenth centuries, it was said, there could be an annual return of 15 to 20 percent, as measured according to the paid-up capital. Most of the merchants belonged to several such trading companies, if only in order to spread the high risks of maritime trade. Frequently those joining together were relatives working at different sites. The methods of bookkeeping were simple. The merchants functioned simultaneously as their own bankers and money changers. Buying and selling on credit was the rule, and the merchants made use of cashless money exchange, using bills of exchange (promissory notes and drafts). Creditworthiness was essential for mercantile success, and merchants observed each other reciprocally and controlled each other indirectly in this way, even though everyone guarded the state of his business as a secret. This form of merchant capitalism was cooperatively molded and closely tied to politics. Common institutions that, like the branch offices, looked after merchants' business tasks collectively, and not only were important strategic decisions made by individual merchants acting on their own, but such decisions were also discussed in the council meetings and governments (political bodies not infrequently dominated by merchants) of the relevant cities and at irregularly scheduled Hanse diets. The longstanding success of the Hanse was equally based on a corporative urban policy that sought out and allocated privileges to individual merchant-entrepreneurs, and which did not shy away from military conflicts if deemed necessary or useful.

Another variant of merchant capitalism that, on the whole, had more dynamism and a more promising future was developed between the twelfth and fifteenth centuries in northern Italian cities (especially Venice, Pisa, Genoa, and Florence) as well as in southern German cities (especially Nuremberg and Augsburg), where the emphasis was also on long-distance trade. This kind of trade required methods for bridging long distances and, if at all possible, without transporting sacks of coins. These projects—perhaps sea journeys lasting several months, often between one and two years, to distant ports, with several intermediate stops and multiple transfers of goods that were new or different each time—kept getting bigger and requiring more capital. Business on the basis of advance payments and credits had already become the rule in Venice as early as the twelfth century, in part on the basis of very high interest rates (20 to 40 percent in the middle of the twelfth century, in some cases). The need for minimizing risk was immense. Several merchants and moneylenders acting as silent partners would join together to form temporary companies. Most conducted business in different lines simultaneously, with different products and functions; there was neither room nor incentive for specialization. Frequently a merchant worked with several ships, while in other cases several owners of capital operated a ship jointly. Profit was sought in order to augment the capital. A large portion of the required capital was generated in the trade itself, but large sums also flowed out of assets acquired politically, even violently, or through agriculture. Large, even huge riches were accumulated, at first (in the twelfth century) only during an individual merchant's lifetime, but later as inherited wealth when one generation shifted to another, and later still with the aim of creating a cross-generational firm. Romano Mairano, an unusually successful shipowner, merchant, and moneylender in Venice between 1150 and 1200 donated what remained of his fortune at the end of his life to the monastery of San Zaccaria (where the papers he bequeathed also survived the centuries). The fortune of the Medici in Florence fluctuated up and down in extreme jumps with the passage of time but was passed on from generation to generation. The Fuggers in Augsburg successfully sought to establish a "house" that, unequivocally family-related, would survive for generations. The formation of *enterprises* with legal personalities of their own—distinct from the household of their shareholders and operators, and moreover often with a variety of changing owners—represents a development in medieval merchant capitalism from the thirteenth century onward, and especially during the fourteenth and fifteenth centuries, that can hardly be overerestimated. It was also a development apparently missing in the versions of merchant capitalism found in China and Arabia. The Great Ravensburg Trading Company, which started in textiles and did business Europe-wide, was supported by more than a hundred families and existed for 150 years (1380–1530).

This expansion of merchant capitalism in the High and Late Middle Ages would not have been possible without the invention of new methods and the deployment of new legal forms. Double-entry bookkeeping, which juxtaposed debit and credit precisely so that both sides of the ledger were instantly retrievable, was known in northern Italian trading cities by the fourteenth century at the latest, and for a long time it was labeled the method *alla Veneziana*. The monitoring instrument of double-entry bookkeeping, however, was not broadly implemented until the nineteenth century. On the whole, this technique proved much less important for the rise of capitalism than scholars like Weber and Sombart assumed. In commercial practice new methods were created, and were soon also introduced as rules and regulations, for handling cashless lending, dealing in promissory notes, and futures trading. This had the effect of expanding, quite decisively, the spatial and temporal dimension within which the business of merchant capitalism could take place. Not only were Arabic-Indian numerals—including zero—adopted from the Orient (around 1200) so as to facilitate written calculations, it also happened that some methods for trading and calculating were copied from Arab competitors and partners. Different legal forms for shareholding, partnership, and capital consolidation were developed, and these rudimentary innovations facilitated capital shares with limited liability (though without an option for trading the shares). The reawakened tradition of Roman law, with its formal rationality and contract-friendly design, was helpful here, even if it did not prove decisive.[10]

In contrast to merchant capitalism in Arabia—and, it would appear, China as well—the southern and western European variants exhibited a striking dynamism; it extended beyond trade, on the one hand in the direction of a financial capitalism with independent institutions and a special closeness to the politically powerful, and on the other hand by penetrating in the first rudimentary way into the world of production.

From the outset, bank transactions—currency exchange, borrowing and lending, business in bills and checks that simplified payment transactions and provided opportunities for profits on their own, including trade in promissory notes starting in the fourteenth century—contained speculative elements. These transactions were settled, to the extent they arose, by the merchants. When these transactions began to increase rapidly in scope, complexity, and importance during the late Middle Ages, they were discharged only to a lesser extent by Jewish or Lombard pawnbrokers, who did exist in large numbers but were mostly engaged in extending consumer credit. They exploited the distress of ordinary people, often charged exorbitant interest, and were denounced as usurers. The majority of those who turned to this new speculative business were merchants, both experienced and aspiring, who were increasingly specializing in financial transactions, even if they did not completely forswear trading in goods. Banks emerged in Genoa starting in the twelfth century, in Venice starting in the thirteenth, and in Tuscany since the beginning of the fourteenth century. Florentine banks—already numbering eighty by 1350—were the most prominent across Europe and remained so until the end of the Middle Ages.

They were mostly organized as family-based trading companies and supported by several partners who deposited the capital, participated in their management, and split the profits. In 1341 the third-largest bank in Florence, the Acciaiuoli Bank, had sixteen branches in different countries, eleven partners, thirty-two managers, and a large number of staff personnel. The Bardis, Peruzzis, and in the fifteenth century the Strozzis and Medicis also attained this stature in the ranks of major transnational companies. They not only made money in the aforementioned business with money, bills, and checks, but they also used their capital, money in accounts deposited with them, and their earnings to acquire shares in and advance credits to trading and commercial enterprises. They also conducted such enterprises on their own. In addition, they issued bonds to city governments, landed and manorial estates, and eventually also to the highest-ranking spiritual and worldly rulers, who were in constant need of money owing to the lack of routine tax revenues and who found it difficult to wage wars, fulfill their ceremonial obligations, and promote their territories' expansion. State formation and the origins of financial capitalism were closely connected, and the nexus provided a way for prosperous urban citizens in high finance, a small elite, to establish their influence on politics while simultaneously making their entrepreneurial success dependent on powerful rulers and their shifting political fortunes.[11]

Through the end of the Middle Ages, capitalism was largely limited to parts of trade and finance. Yet early on, merchant capital *selectively* pushed out beyond the sphere of distribution. This happened both in the mining business, with its huge capital requirements and often quite extensive plant operations based on wage labor, and in cottage industry. Here and there, merchants began to exercise influence over the production of goods they intended to market by advancing raw materials to producers, placing orders, and sometimes also providing tools. Examples may be found above all in the history of the wool trade in northern Italy (here, again, especially in Florence) and in the Netherlands (Flanders, Brabant), starting in the thirteenth century at the latest. As a result, there was a change in the division of labor among producers. Their dependence on the market and its fluctuations increased tangibly. Their status became closer to that of the wage worker, since they remained formally independent but were actually receiving piecework wages, sometimes in the form of advances they were required to work off. This often turned the merchant into a "factor" (*Verleger*) and the craftsman into a homeworker or cottage laborer. Workshop labor and hourly rate work also took place. This led to a sharp increase in a number of tensions, between capital and direct producers, between merchants and artisans, and between entrepreneurs and workers. These tensions sometimes fed the tumults and uprisings that frequently took place in commercially developed areas during the fourteenth century (even if these disturbances also had other causes), for example the *tumulto dei ciompi* in Florence in 1378, which was settled by force of arms and suppressed with the aid of city authorities. Not always did the rudiments of cottage industry—which could also be found in other lines of business, as in the Nuremberg metal trade, the linen industry in Constance, and in southern Italian ship construction—lead to open conflicts. Yet it became apparent early on that the social explosiveness of capitalism increased as soon as it began to expand from the sphere of circulation to the sphere of production and to reshape the world of work directly.[12]

To the extent that it was catching on, then, capitalism in the European Middle Ages was sustained by merchants. They encompassed very different livelihoods: from prosperous, respected, and long-established patricians with extended families and membership in the city regiment to Jewish or Lombard moneychangers who were denounced as usurers and lived in great insecurity on the fringes of society; from deeply entrenched members of an influential guild to the occasional merchant or the freshly risen nouveau riche; from the rich merchant-banker who associated on friendly terms with highest-ranking power holders to the exhausted traveling agent who routinely visited suppliers and producers in a proletarianized milieu and served as a messenger passing on information. But an orientation toward profit, experience in handling money, and the ability to compete in markets was something they all had in common, even if they knew how to value the advantages of monopolies and aspired to privileges, that is, sought favors from the politically powerful and ways to shield themselves against the vagaries of the market. Most of the merchants in wholesale and long-distance trade were among the educated of their time, since they could read, write, and count. Their supraregional orientation, which came out of their experience in long-distance trade, lent many of them a certain cosmopolitanism. The inherently uncertain yet malleable nature of their business saw to it that entrepreneurial, ambitious, success-hungry, bold persons were strongly attracted to this field and disproportionally represented in it. Strikingly, too, these merchants—if only because demand was limited and sales, as a rule, were small—did not specialize. They traded with many and took care of a variety of business at the same time, paying attention to what was on offer or just coming on the market, and they looked for opportunities, hardly squeamish about the dangers that constituted the norm in a world where there was little in the way of any "stateness" as soon as one left the relatively guarded space of one's walled-in city and the familiar surroundings of one's local community. Failure was frequent. Even large and long-successful enterprises went bankrupt. There was no lack of stories about the decline of great families from positions of wealth and power. These merchants and bankers were far from being able to settle comfortably into specialized and manageable routines. In the struggle for commercial success, they had to be alert and cautious, even suspicious, and, from time to time, unscrupulous. They knew pride in individual accomplishment. They took advantage of self-interest with toughness. A certain inclination to secretiveness was also involved. They were not acting as civic matadors of an early bourgeois public realm. They strove after money, not in order to hoard it, but rather to let it work and multiply. All this fit in with capitalist principles.

But, in contrast to the more fully developed capitalism that would come later, the fixed capital tied up in trade remained limited by nature, and capital accumulation happened neither quickly nor in unlimited fashion. One reason for this, in spite of sometimes very high profit rates, was that only a portion of the profits were used to expand the typical undertaking, which in any event was planned in the main to last for only a few years and could rarely be assumed to survive the death of the originating merchant. Often, a large portion of the profits from an undertaking went into consumption, even (or especially) into luxury consumption or into the acquisition of real estate. Land at that time represented a durable foundation that could be inherited by the next generation, in contrast to the temporary character of merchant capital, which did not survive the times. Altogether, this fit in with the era's notions of the good bourgeois life in which, with growing economic success and advanced age, one sought to replace the excitement of a trader's business with the leisurely existence of a pensioner, and in addition to acquire a comfortable country home. One might even, as in the case of a few especially successful merchants, seek to add a noble title, an acquisition generally held in high regard, and ownership of a manor or castle. In other words, under the social and cultural conditions of the Middle Ages, capital accumulation and entrepreneurial growth were a long way from being the dominant goals they later became. Instead, profit and business success remained a means to the end of the good life.

It needs to be made clear that even this moderate variant of capitalist practice could only catch on at a certain remove from deeply rooted moral ideas. Not only did the doctrine of the Christian Church prohibit moneylending, extending credit for interest being regarded as "usury," at least if it was lending to "thy brother" (i.e. member of one's own tribe, group, or religion), as said in Deuteronomy (23:20, KJV). Interest-bearing lending from Christians to other Christians was, to this extent, prohibited, which largely explains the strong representation of Jews in such transactions. The Christian doctrine, which had originated in an agricultural-artisanal milieu, where solidarity was esteemed as a form of fraternity, undoubtedly gave expression to widespread anticapitalist attitudes. These attitudes rejected profit as a lifetime goal, and they evoked mistrust of the merchant's livelihood. With time, these attitudes did soften, or they were interpreted in such a way that they could be reconciled with economic reality as it unfolded. There were, moreover, many methods of getting around the prohibition on interest and on making credit transactions accessible to Christians, too. The church's moral doctrine also developed countervailing arguments that interpreted exchange, profit, and prosperity as legitimate compensation for the financial insecurities and difficulties merchants faced, and as useful for the public welfare.

But it is still remarkable that capitalism was able to catch on in a Christian-influenced medieval Europe only against the obstacles of widespread mistrust, moral rejection, and intellectual criticism. Merchants accommodated such attitudes, to some extent, by adopting a lifestyle and imagery compatible with religion, by donating heavily to charity, and often also by making a "final penance" in old age through large transfers of wealth to monasteries and churches. Anxiety about the torments of hell is also certain to have shaped the spiritual attitude of many medieval merchants, most of whom, in spite of all their worldliness, were devoted Christians. Yet the dynamism of merchant capitalism was hardly dampened by the anticapitalism of Christian-influenced public morality, just as the ever-present ideological critique of capitalism in centuries to come only rarely interfered with the spread of capitalism as a practical matter.[13]

Interim Findings around 1500

In the millennium between 500 and 1500, merchant capitalism was a global and not a specifically European phenomenon. Beyond the cases of China, Arabia, and Europe depicted here, it also existed in other regions of the world, for example in India and Southeast Asia.[14] It evidently developed under very different social, cultural, and religious conditions. In the comparative perspective of global history, Europe was a latecomer that remained backward for a long time as far as the formation of the institutions of capitalism and its behaviors is concerned.

The many types of capitalism in the world regions discussed here, in China, Arabia, and Europe, did not exist in isolation from each other. Rather, they were aware of and influenced each other, even as early as the period regarded in the West as the High Middle Ages. As far as the history of these types of capitalism is concerned, it was Europe that learned and adopted more from the others than the other way around. But the linkages were not intensive enough so that one could speak of a "world system" as early as the era around 1200 or 1300.[15] Even if capitalist development in Europe lagged behind that of China and Arabia, it did soon appear to be the most dynamic of the three. This is most clearly demonstrated by the way Europe seized on a kind of capitalism that was initially characterized above all by long-distance trade but slowly expanded into other areas: into an emerging financial system that included the financing of political powers as well as into the sphere of production, above all in cottage industry. Why? Explanations from the history of religion can be ruled out. For the moral teachings of Christianity impeded the way to capitalism's beginnings in medieval Europe more decisively and with greater inhibition than was done by Islam since the seventh century in Arabia and by the East Asian religions since the tenth century in China. Nor can the exploitation of non-European resources by Europe be invoked as an explanatory factor for the period prior to 1500. Undoubtedly, different factors played a role. Yet what proved decisive was the relationship between the economy and the state, between market processes and political power, at least in a Sino-European comparison. And indeed, this distinctive relationship between economics and politics was already characteristic of the early phase that preceded European expansion into other parts of the world.

Neither in China nor in Europe nor anywhere else did merchant capitalism develop at a clear remove from those who exercised political power, and nowhere in all those centuries did a clear *differentiation* between the economy and the state emerge. Both in China and in Europe (and to some extent in Arabia) there were close interconnections between the economic power of the merchants and the political power of the authorities. State formation and market formation were jumbled together everywhere. But in Europe the political system was intrinsically diverse and positively fragmented, while in China there was a centralized empire. The hard, frequently warlike competition between city-states, principalities, territorial states, and other political units was a central part of the European, but not of the

Chinese, configuration. At the same time, European cities had a great deal of civic political autonomy that was lacking in Chinese cities. It followed logically from the European configuration that those exercising political rule competed with each other to promote economic potential in the territories they governed, while this motive did not animate China's civil service governments as much and receded even further into the background during the fifteenth century. The merchants who supported capitalism in Europe, or at least their leading representatives, exercised direct influence on politics—in part via a symbiosis with rulers in the city-states and free cities that had civic rule, in part through close ties to those exercising political power and in need of financial support, in part through formal self-organization (guilds). By contrast, merchants in China, as well as in Arabia and India, were confined to the antechamber of power and were much less engaged in financing state formation than was the case in Europe. This explains how, in the final analysis and in spite of many countervailing trends, politics in Europe was decisive for promoting mercantile dynamism and a capitalistic kind of accumulation. By contrast, Chinese politics, although it initially allowed and supported commercial dynamism and major developments in accumulating large amounts of capital to inch forward a bit, then became strong enough and mistrustful enough to restrain both of these trends so that finally, when both domestic and foreign policy changed, these economic forces were ultimately thwarted.[16]

So far, the development of capitalism in trade, and especially in long-distance trade, has essentially been depicted in a way that showed how merchants and their undertakings played the decisive role. While it has proven impossible to pinpoint clear starting dates, the tenth through fourteenth century in China, seventh through eleventh century in Arabia, and the twelfth through fifteenth century in Europe have turned out to be reliable dates bookmarking phases of accelerated expansion. Those in the Marxist tradition who will only speak of capitalism when capitalist principles are guiding *production* and shaping the way work is organized there tend to categorize the phenomena just discussed as precapitalist.[17] I do not share this point of view. These early merchants' intense relationship to the market and their strong profit orientation, the relative independence enjoyed by commercial actions and institutions, the significance of investment and accumulation that used credit and were profit oriented, the formation of enterprise (at least in Europe), and finally the dynamic way that capitalist developments radiated beyond long-distance trade (at least in Europe), even into the rudiments of production—all this justifies and compels categorizing these phenomena as capitalist in the meaning of the definition established at the outset of this book. There were also causal relationships. The merchant capitalism (or commercial capitalism) of those earlier centuries generated capital, techniques, and connections that took effect in those later variants of capitalism that did incorporate the sphere of production more thoroughly.

Yet it is clear that, in many respects, we are dealing only with the rudiments of capitalism and not with capitalism in the full meaning of the definition established at the outset of this book. As a rule, a thoroughly capitalistic organization of production did not take place, either in agriculture or in trade and manufacture. The frequently attested reluctance of important actors to engage in capital investment and accumulation posed an additional limitation, no matter how interesting and meaningful it may be, particularly in light of current problems, to reconstruct how this reluctance came about. It did, after all, signify how capitalism was socially embedded and politically regulated. Finally, there is something that cannot be emphasized strongly enough even though it could not be made sufficiently clear in the preceding account: that the manifestations of capitalism depicted in that account were *minority phenomena*, all taking place while the economy and society functioned by and large according to noncapitalist principles. Overall, subsistence and domestic economies prevailed in many medieval societies, a large part of economic interactions took place without reference to markets, noneconomic forms of dependence and domination were paramount, and inequality was largely determined by politics and social status. This chapter was mostly about islands of capitalism in a predominantly noncapitalist environment. These islands could crumble away again, as in the Chinese case; teleological ways of thinking about this are not apposite. Yet on the whole these islands grew, and the effects that emanated from them expanded.

3

Expansion

Until around 1500, capitalism appeared on the scene primarily as merchant capitalism, in which form its impact on economy and society was rather limited overall. In the following three centuries, however, a fundamental broadening of capitalism took place: it expanded spatially into the newly established world trading system, crossed new frontiers into the sphere of production, and became important for society as a whole, especially in the Netherlands and England. How it was evaluated by the public changed, mainly for the better. In this phase, which from a European perspective is regarded as the early modern era, western Europe clearly became the leading region in the history of capitalism, even if global integration was on the increase at the same time. The rise of capitalism, the development of powerful territorial states, and the expansion of Europe that led to colonialism were all contingent on each other.

Business and Violence: Colonialism and World Trade

According to Marx, modern capitalism came into the world soaked in blood and filth, as the result of violence and suppression.[1] This is only a half-truth historically, but nonetheless a correct observation when one considers the connection between the rise of capitalism and colonization. What is often euphemistically called the Age of Discovery was in reality an age of subjugation, part violent and part commercial, of a large part of the world by European powers. Portuguese and Spaniards traversed the Atlantic and plundered the treasures of the South American empires. While destroying the Aztec, Incan, and Mayan empires, they also took away control of the seaway to Asia from the Arabs, after opening the route around the southern tip of Africa, and transformed numerous ports on the coasts of this continent into European bases. This sixteenth-century southern European "crown capitalism" (Wolfgang Reinhard) was followed in the seventeenth century by the merchant capitalism of the Dutch, who established a colonial empire in Southeast Asia and contended with the French and English for influence in North America and Africa. The English won this battle, and after numerous wars with the Spanish and French in the eighteenth century, vaulted to the position of leading colonial power. With the aid of a powerful fleet, the newly dominant English procured lucrative trade, established settlements, and exercised rule in a variety of ways, usually indirect, from North America to the Indian subcontinent and Australia. Other European countries tried to keep up, though on the whole in vain: the gap between western Europe and the rest of the continent became deeper. Around 1500, European powers controlled about 7 percent of the world's territory, but by 1775 this was 35 percent.

It would not be correct to interpret this spectacular expansion exclusively as the logical consequence of European

capitalism. Ranking very high among the driving forces behind this expansion were the claims asserted by territorial
states in the midst of consolidating their power and by
their governments. Christian missionary goals also played
a role, albeit less as motivating forces than as legitimation
for political and economic expansion. But economic interests—the aspiration to riches and profit, the hunger for
precious metals, the pursuit of trade advantages in order
to prevail in the intense competition with other European powers—were crucial impetuses behind this European
protrusion into the world. Accordingly, the great expeditions and acquisitions of land were, in general, undertaken
by independently operating conquistadors, entrepreneurs,
captains, adventurers, and merchants who combined the
military with the commercial. Thus, conquistadors like
Hernán Cortés obtained substantial loans prior to their departure in order to procure the weapons they needed and
make sure they could pay their people. Operating at the
heart of the European expansion into the world was a dynamic symbiosis between ambitious holders of political
power, calculating financiers, and daring or perhaps unscrupulous adventurers. Here we see an irritating amalgamation of trade and warfare, an aggressive jumble of lust
for power, capitalist dynamism, and lawless violence. This
mix did not become the rule historically, but it keeps crop-
ping up, even in the present.[2]

The effects of this configuration on the further development of capitalism were immense. A new world trade system emerged, with western Europe as its center. The gold
and silver in South America that was initially plundered,
then massively exploited in the mines there, found its way
into international commerce as a means of payment. As

currency, these precious metals precipitated inflation in Europe, and for the most part they ended up in the temples and palaces of Asia, for this was the only way that Europeans (who apart from weapons, had little to export that would have been of interest to Indians on the subcontinent and to the Chinese) could pay for the permanent stream of Asian luxury goods now flowing into Europe. The mostly Dutch and English trading companies, shipowners, and sea captains developed the triangular trade that was characteristic of Atlantic commerce well into the eighteenth century: they brought goods for mass consumption (especially textiles, metal utensils, and weapons) from Europe to ports along the African West Coast. From there they transported Africans as slaves to America, where most of this human cargo was highly coveted as cheap labor in the developing plantation economy of Brazil, the Caribbean, and the southern regions of North America. Finally, they transported sugar, tobacco, cotton, and other American export goods to Europe, where these were sold at a profit, processed into finished goods, and consumed. Older trade networks in which Asian and African merchants had played a larger role were suppressed and destroyed.

Inside Europe, moreover, there developed a lively trade that brought agricultural surpluses, especially grain, from eastern and east central Europe into the western regions of the continent, where urbanization was proceeding apace, export business was on the rise, and demand was growing. This shifted the centers of gravitation for long-distance trade inside Europe; the Mediterranean lost what the Atlantic gained in importance. Correspondingly, the leading regions of capitalist development inside Europe wandered, initially from northern Italy, southern Germany, and the Baltic–North Sea region to the Netherlands, and then to England. So that it was no longer Genoa and Florence, Augsburg and Lübeck, but increasingly Antwerp, then Amsterdam, and finally London that became centers of the world economy. Without a doubt, this increasingly intense long-distance trade generated big profits and had a considerable impact on demand: it was a crucial motor driving the export-oriented plantation economy in the colonies and establishing capitalism in agriculture, industry, and consumption in western Europe.[3]

Joint-Stock Company and Finance Capitalism

The combination of merchant capitalism and expanding colonialism gave rise to organizational innovations. On the one hand, the *enterprise*, as a core institutional component of capitalism as it was taking shape, attained a much clearer profile than ever before. The 1602 Dutch "United East India Company" (in old Dutch spelling the Vereenigde Oostindische Compagnie, or VOC) was the most important in a long series of joint-stock companies that emerged in the sixteenth and seventeenth centuries in several countries for the purpose of colonial trade, especially in the Netherlands, England, and France. On the other hand, new types of institutions and practices of finance capitalism emerged that are active to this day. For example, there have been stock exchanges trading in securities in Antwerp since 1531, in Amsterdam since 1611–1612, and in London since 1698.

Trade enterprises had already existed, but through the sixteenth century primarily as partnerships that brought together a small number of merchants working and keeping accounts relatively independently. The VOC, however, came into being as a public corporation. Its impressive capital of 6.45 million guilders was raised by 219 shareholders, each with limited liability. They regularly received dividends (18 percent on average annually) but had little influence on the management of the company. The VOC stayed together until 1799, while its shareholders changed. They could do this because they could trade their shares on the newly emerging stock exchanges. This made belonging to an enterprise tradable on markets. Entry and exit were made easier. The management of the company lay in the hands of directors. They ran the extensive, vertically integrated organization and its many branch offices (especially in Asia) out of Amsterdam with the aid of an ingenious system of committees, a systemic reporting system, and a central office that soon employed a staff of 350 salaried employees. The company operated the purchase, transport, and sale of a variety of goods. But it also expanded selectively to become a manufacturing company by incorporating, for example, saltpeter works and silk-spinning plants in India.

In all these respects, the VOC seemed unusually modern. Yet what distinguished it from the huge multinational enterprises that were to come in the nineteenth and twentieth centuries was its character as a monopoly with extensive quasi-governmental powers. The States-General of the Netherlands' United Provinces had a government that conferred on the VOC the right to operate all Dutch trading business east of the Cape of Good Hope, along with the authorization "to wage war, conclude treaties, take possession of land, and build fortresses." The VOC exercised these rights, often in armed struggle with competitors from other countries. The transition between conducting capitalist business and waging war was fluid. There were years in which the company apparently drew the major share of its income from the seizure of competing or enemy ships.

The huge capital requirements and complexity of services to be performed are not the only factors explaining the emergence of this unique organization. The Dutch East India Company also fit in with the political needs of government in this era, since business, politics, and military force were most intimately mixed, and intensive competition between states often brought to a standstill competition between enterprises within one and the same country. The VOC was formed as an alliance of merchants and trading companies from all the provinces of the Netherlands under pressure from the government, as a pooling of resources in international competition with an anti-Spanish, and then soon also an anti-English, thrust. Much the same can be said of other trading companies of the time, such as the much smaller English East India Company, which existed between 1600 and 1858, but also the Dutch West-India Company and comparable establishments, for example in Scandinavian countries.[4]

Transactions in money, bills of exchange, transfers, credit, and insurance were part of merchant capitalism from the outset, at least in Europe. They were undertaken not only by the merchants who were primarily dealing in commodities; increasingly, too, since the twelfth century, they were also undertaken by banks that specialized in these transactions but were also operating internationally and usually also taking deposits while charging interest, either openly or concealed. Early on in these transactions, a major role was played by loans to city governments, manorial estates, territorial sovereigns, princes, and kings, all the way up to the (Holy Roman) Emperor and the pope. Thus, the business magnate Jacob Fugger, who came from a family of weavers and traders in Augsburg, was not only trading in a wide range of goods and operating mining companies, but also running a major bank. In this role he helped finance the election, wars, and other state affairs of the Habsburg emperors Kaiser Maximilian I und Charles V. Both as merchant and banker, Fugger did not fare badly. In the final decade of his life, his business achieved an average profit of 54 percent per annum. When he died in 1525, he was certainly Europe's richest entrepreneur. In seventeenth-century England, too, the largest fortunes were made in financial transactions, not by trading in goods.[5]

Increasingly, the center of this densely networked finance capitalism shifted to western Europe. The instruments of commercial traffic in transfers and bills of exchange originally developed in Italy were developed further in Antwerp, Amsterdam, and London, where they were adapted to new needs by an ever-growing number of banks.

The shares of the monopoly companies engaged in colonial business represented a considerable portion of the commercial paper traded on the stock exchanges. Capital increasingly became a commodity, and the speculative elements associated with it grew by leaps and bounds. Not only did the prospect of spectacular profits increase thereby, but so did the danger of great losses. Both the opportunities and perils soon affected not just a small number of active, professional trade capitalists but an increasing number of small and large investors from wide sections of the population in western European metropolises as well. In the course of the seventeenth century, these new investors learned how to try their luck on the stock exchange, to bet, invest, and speculate. As early as the beginning of the seventeenth century, more than a thousand interested parties had initially registered in order to acquire shares in the VOC, only eighty of them with more than 10,000 guilders, most with quite modest sums. In the second half of the seventeenth century, the main investors in Dutch government paper came from "all groups of the population, among which were great banks, the town oligarchies, insurance companies, the middle classes (including those in the liberal professions, officials and lesser annuitants), prosperous members of the farming community, and institutional investors (including both religious communities and charitable organisations)" (van der Wee).[6] The downfall of the English South Sea Company in 1720 was preceded by a full-fledged speculation mania. The British government had granted the company a monopoly on trade with South America, including all the rights to regions not yet discovered! The public was expecting an imminent political weakening of Spain and, as a consequence, gigantic profits from this transaction. A run on shares set in, and the share price rose from £120 to £905 within just a month. Broad segments of the population entrusted their money to the company and lost it when the bubble burst in the summer and the share price went into free fall. Sir Isaac Newton was among the victims. He is supposed to have said: "I can calculate the motions of erratic stars, but not the madness

of the multitude." The macroeconomic and social consequences of such crises did remain quite limited. Yet, via
the stock market and speculation, entire classes of society
got their first introduction to the hopes and disappoint-
ments, the gains and losses, that capitalism so abundantly
held in store for them. There is food for thought and study
in the history of company bankruptcies that frequently
happened even back then.[7]

The early modern rise of the banks did not result merely
from the growing credit needs of expanding trade and the
ensuing demand for newfangled brokerage and transfer
services. Rather, the services provided by banks were deliberately requested by those in power. Quite early on, it was
city governments wanting these financial services, but
then later it was above all the governments of powerful
territorial states just establishing themselves. These emerging states required much more funding than was available
from their own revenues to wage their numerous wars,
put their power and prestige on display, and expand their
lands. By using the banks, they could attempt to skim off
for their own purposes a portion of those private and corporate assets to which the banks had access as deposits or
loans. Furthermore, they used large trading houses to col-
lect tariffs and taxes. Time and time again, they were in-
debted to the capitalists, and occasionally they used their
political clout to compel debt relief. They offered their
creditors, in addition to high interest rates, such privileges
as monopolies or mining rights, official recognition, and—
in case of victory at war—a share in the booty. Via sub-
scriptions to bonds and loans floated or secured by states

and municipalities, many different groups—members of the middle and upper classes but also corporative and co-operative institutions such as church congregations and foundations—now had their economic livelihood tied to the polity that governed them.

As a result of this configuration, the very large profits, but also the not-infrequent collapses of enterprises, came to depend not only on market success and failure but also on the fate and capriciousness of political powers. But the configuration looked different in different countries. What proved decisive was how public debt was regulated in the long run. The Dutch Republic and the English constitutional monarchy established after 1688–1689 succeeded in consolidating the public debt, for which the (Dutch) States-Provincial and States-General or the (London) Parliament, and thus also the representatives of the financially potent population groups politically enfranchised in the Netherlands and England, were answerable.

Against this background, the creditworthiness and economic power of the Netherlands and England grew considerably, and incidentally also the power and room for maneuvering of the governments there to increase taxes and simultaneously maintain a large public debt at acceptable rates of interest. The Netherlands succeeded in continuing to play a key role in banking and finance for Europe and the world even after its dynamism as a center of merchant capitalism began to wane in the eighteenth century. An ingredient in the successful renewal of public finances in England was the creation in 1694 of the Bank of England, which was organized by the private sector but quickly became a kind of central bank, assumed the role of "lender of last resort," and helped shape the country's monetary policy: it made an important contribution to state formation and to the further development of capitalism as well.

Plantation Economy and Slavery

"It would seem that almost all elements of financial apparatus that we've come to associate with capitalism—central banks, bond markets, short-selling, brokerage houses, speculative bubbles, securitization, annuities—came into being not only before the science of economics (which is perhaps not too surprising), but also before the rise of factories, and wage labor itself."[8] And, indeed, around 1750 capitalism had become established in western Europe as merchant and finance capitalism, without any profound capitalist reorganization of the sphere of production having taken place. That thorough reorganization came with industrialization, which began in England in the second half of the eighteenth century (see chapter 4 below). Yet even before industrialization started, capitalism did not leave the sphere of production totally untouched. The following is an outline of the most important arenas in which capitalism rearranged the sphere of production even prior to industrialization: plantation labor, agriculture, mining and protoindustrial manufacture.

Whoever is accustomed to associating capitalism with "doubly free wage labor"—labor free of noneconomic compulsion and free of the means of production, recruited and paid on a contractual basis, and paid within the framework of an exchange relationship of labor power against wages—must first get used to the irritating idea that the triumph of early modern capitalism outside Europe and also, to an extent, in the eastern half of the European continent led to a massive *increase in unfree labor*. The exploitation of South American silver mines by the Portuguese and Spanish in the sixteenth century was already largely based on forced labor into which the native Indians were pressed, from which they suffered, and as a result of which they often died. From the late sixteenth century to the late seventeenth century, the colony of Brazil, first Dutch and then Portuguese, was the world's largest producer of sugar, primarily for export to Europe. First tobacco and then, as in Brazil, sugar were exported in large quantities from the Caribbean, a region fought over by the colonial powers. Initially, for example, sugar was exported from Barbados, and this continued well into the 1820s. Planters in Virginia and South Carolina took up the production and export of tobacco, rice, indigo, and then especially, starting in the late eighteenth century, cotton. The massive cultivation of these staple commodities produced for export came about as a consequence of colonization and resulted primarily from initiatives and investments of European merchants and trading companies, as well as—increasingly—agrarian entrepreneurs in the land who had migrated there. The system operated across boundaries and was a product of capitalism.

Production took place largely in the plantation system, which also came to be used over the centuries in other parts of the world, as in India, Southeast Asia, and parts of Africa. Plantations were large agricultural concerns that specialized in the production of high-quality staple commodities for export, not infrequently as monocultural cultivation. The capital investment needed for the plantation economy was considerable. The value of a medium-large sugar cane plantation with 240 hectares and 200 slaves in Jamaica in 1770 was put at £19,000: 37.5 percent of the capital was allotted to slaves, 31.5 percent to land, and 21 percent to the sugar cane mill. The profits were said to have amounted to as much as 50 percent at the outset, and in the eighteenth century they oscillated between 5 and 10 percent.

In light of the scarcity and insufficient suitability of native workers, African, European and American slave traders sold between 11 and 12 million Africans, both men and women, to America, from the sixteenth through the nineteenth century. Of these, the West Indies took 48 percent, Brazil 38 percent, and the southern regions of what later became the United States of America barely 5 percent. By far the largest share of them landed, at least initially, in plantations, while others served as household slaves, artisans, or in other jobs that changed but were always determined by the owner.

Working alongside the slaves at the plantations, especially in the southern British colonies since the seventeenth century, were numerous "indentured servants" who, typically in return for getting a free trans-Atlantic crossing from Europe, were obligated to perform labor service, usually for five to ten years, so that they were also unfree laborers, though for a limited period of time. Other laborers received a wage or salary on a contractual, terminable basis. This was especially true of the supervisors, who were quite numerous on the plantations in order to guarantee

tough discipline for the workforce, which was mostly organized in gangs and which was often worn out to its limits. The plantation economy was typically committed to
strict calculation and a goal-oriented organization of work,
yet at the same time it could deplete resources without
any regard to the future. For, given the superabundance of
land, and so long as able-bodied slaves could be acquired
cheaply, the plantations put no weight (at least not initially) on the sustainability of either land or labor.

From the perspective provided by the history of capitalism, two things should be emphasized. On the one hand,
the plantation economy demonstrated in exemplary fashion how capitalism on the rise can fundamentally reshape
the sphere of production via demand and investment,
workforce recruitment, and management, without consis-
tently implementing its most important principles—in
this case, the principle of exchange and the commodity
form—into the organization of labor. For, during the phase
of their enslavement, transport, and sale to their new owners, slaves were indeed made into a commodity in an extreme, humanly debasing manner, a commodity exchanged
between slave hunter, slave trader, and plantation operator.
Yet on the plantation the relationship between slaveholder
and slave was not one in which labor power was exchanged
for wages between formally equal participants in a labor
market, rather it was a relationship of extreme inequality
between owner and property. Capitalism is evidently compatible—at least for a time and under *certain conditions*—
with different ways of organizing and exploiting work. This
holds true to this day. In the case of the early modern colonial plantation economy with slave labor, *these conditions*

included the enterprise's concentration on relatively homogenous staple commodities requiring a great deal of unskilled work, a still poorly developed labor market, and highly charged cultural and racial differences between capitalists and entrepreneurs on the one hand and workers on the other.

The efficiency of the slave economy remained limited. While owners wanted to get as much output as they could from their slaves, the latter often kept their output deliberately low due to lack of motivation and latent resistance. "Occasionally, resistance was manifested in insubordination, sabotage, murder attempts, and uprisings punished with demonstrative gruesomeness by the white minority facing an African majority" (Reinhard). It is unlikely that a more diversified agriculture, or any business based on diversified skills, and later industrialization would have been possible in the long run on the basis of slave labor. But plantation slavery remained highly profitable as late as the nineteenth century in Brazil (coffee), Cuba (sugar), and the southern states of the USA (cotton), as well as in many other places. The employment of slaves was not, as has been repeatedly claimed, abandoned owing to its economic inferiority; rather, between 1833 (Great Britain) and 1888 (Brazil), it was banned under political pressure, as the result of religious-humanitarian commitment and the reform movements fed by dedication to that cause.

Slavery has a long tradition in many regions of the world. In the eighteenth century there were as many slaves in Africa itself as in America. But under the influence of capitalism, slavery not only increased enormously in scope; it also, in connection with the harsh work discipline typically appertaining to this economic system, took on a special brutality. One cannot say that capitalism would not have developed further without its centuries-long connection to slavery. Nor is it a tenable thesis to claim that industrialization since the late eighteenth century was fed by the gigantic profits of the slave trade, as incontestable as the multiplier effects are that emanated from it into other branches of trade, the textile business, shipbuilding, and other sectors of the economy in western European countries. But if one wants to understand what it means to say that capitalism came into the world bloody and dirty, it is necessary to keep an eye on its relationship to slavery and other forms of unfree labor. This piece of its history shows, moreover, that capitalism of its own accord contains little in the way of resistance against inhumane practices, but that it is compatible with such resistance when subjected to legal-political restrictions and guidance.[9]

Agrarian Capitalism, Mining, and Proto-Industrialization

It would be absolutely wrong to imagine the medieval and early modern *agricultural economy in Europe* as a self-contained and stagnating system. Rather, ever since the expansion of cities in the High Middle Ages there was a division of labor and thus also trade between town and country, even if mostly small-scale and elemental. Across the centuries, agriculture experienced profound crises and distinct boom phases, food prices differed regionally and oscillated over the course of time, and the lifetime opportunities for agricultural producers differed and oscillated along with the price fluctuations. There was pronounced inequality between regions, between estates and farms large and small, between lords, free peasants, and an underclass of the rural poor and landless, usually very dependent and mostly imperiled in the majority, who in many regions constituted the greater part of the agricultural labor force. This was all associated with countless conflicts, protests, and acts of repression. Land was not only inherited, stolen, and newly apportioned but also traded on market terms, even if under restrictive rules that varied strongly by region. Over the centuries, there was progress in agricultural working methods. Productivity in agriculture grew slowly, though interrupted by long-lasting retrogressive phases and characterized by large regional differences. The agricultural-rural world was never safe and sound, and never in a tranquil state.

Agriculture, in which the great majority of people were still doing most of their work and earning most of their living, was certainly not traditional territory for capitalism. Self-sufficiency was widespread, meaning that households, farms, and estates produced the greatest share of what people living there consumed, so that people were involved in markets only in a supplementary way and quite marginally. In the rural-agricultural world, orientation to what was traditional was quite pronounced, thinking in categories of innovation and growth hardly so. The village, almost everywhere the prevailing social form, was—for all its inequality—a force that strengthened communality instead of individualization and competition, personal exchange instead of anonymous market relationships, tradition ahead of critique.

In the greater part of Europe it was feudalism, above all, that stood in the way of capitalist arrangements. Because of the way it tightly linked economic and social relations and defined both prerogatives and dependencies not only economically, but above all socially and politically, feudalism severely limited market exchange as a regulating mechanism. It effectively restricted the economic room for maneuver, in both thought and action, to all social strata: lords of the manor, peasants, and members of the rural lower class. It braked the dynamism of change that can result from new goods and services, from investment and accumulation of profits, as well as from an orientation toward competition and growth. Between the lord of the manor or estate and "his" peasants, cottagers, and farmhands there was a multilayered system of privileges and dependencies. That system equipped the lord with political rights, but also with welfare obligations, that went far beyond the rights and obligations of an employer in the capitalist system; it obligated the subjects, unlike free peasants and unlike agricultural wageworkers later on, to provide the lord with tributes and services (frequently in the form of extended corvée labor); and it restricted the freedom of economic actors, for example by tying them to the land. There was *dominium directum* ("direct ownership" or "superiority") and *dominium utile* ("ownership of use" or "beneficial ownership"), that is, there were entangled property rights of lords and subjects with respect to the same piece of land. These overlapping property rights existed alongside village common property (common lands, communal open fields) for the use of all the villagers, especially the poorest. Mostly, one and the same region contained farms bound to either manorial or estate rule alongside estates owned by free peasants alongside dependent peasants who were under the jurisdiction of the sovereign. The system was complex and varied from region to region. It could, especially in western Europe, become largely monetized—taxes instead of tributes and services—and a bit commercialized, by incorporating leasing relationships. But it could also, further east in Europe, merge into harsh forms of estate rule in which the lord operated a self-sufficient estate while also demanding corvée labor, at the same time that his subjects' ties to the land took on a compulsory character and hardened into "serfdom.[10]

It is remarkable that elements of capitalism did, after all, nestle themselves within this world of old European agriculture, averted as it was from capitalist principles, and that this implantation of capitalist components within the feudal system happened step by step over a long period of time; without exception, it happened in close association with trade, which opened up sales opportunities for agricultural producers, opportunities that served as incentives for them to restructure relations of production; but mostly this process of making agriculture more capitalist was also taking place under the influence of government intervention that either promoted the penetration of capitalism into agriculture or attempted to protect farming from the consequences of that penetration (as in the eighteenth century *Bauernschutz*, the Prussian state's edicts for protection of the peasantry). The export-oriented but feudally integrated agrarian capitalism of eastern central and eastern Europe, which became prevalent starting in the sixteenth century, proved astonishingly durable. Agricultural estates in East Elbian Germany, in Poland, Bohemia, and Hungary, and in the Baltics produced staple commodities, especially grain, for profitable export to western Europe at the same time

that, at home, they tightened the bonds tying their peasants and other subjects on their estates to the land and
"cleared" peasants, thereby expanding the size of their estates that were self-sufficient and intensifying exploitation
through corvée labor. This came to be known as a *second
serfdom*. It was an export-oriented agrarian capitalism on
the basis of unfree labor and noncapitalist organization of
work that recalls the capitalist-oriented plantation system
based on slave labor. It exercised great social and political
influence, in Prussia for example, and survived in an altered form even after the peasant liberation of the early
nineteenth century had removed the legal foundations of
the "second serfdom."[11] This large-scale agrarian capitalism
based on unfree labor developed in areas with a strong feudal tradition, low degree of urbanization, and poorly developed local market relations. The estate lords concluded
contracts with long-distance trade merchants who transported their goods through ports like Königsberg, Danzig,
or Stettin to consumers in western Europe, while individual peasants whose freedom was strongly restricted barely
had direct access to markets in their immediate vicinity.
There was also no strong territorial sovereign who could
have put limits on the ruthless interest politics of the feudal lords who were conducting business capitalistically.

Capitalism became prevalent in the agricultural economy of the Netherlands in a wholly different manner.
There the feudal traditions were weak, the degree of urbanization high, and demand for agricultural products strong.
In hindsight one can discern very continuous market relations that were deepening. Town-country trade relations
that intensified early on stimulated specialization in agricultural production, resulting in market integration that

continued to grow and, when surpluses accrued, in growing long-distance trade as well. Landed property was bought, sold, and leased. A regional capital market developed. Burghers used considerable capital to acquire stakes in flourishing farmsteads run by prosperous peasants who invested and accumulated, showed interest in improving cultivation methods and developed new products, while other, mostly smaller farmsteads with insecure property rights declined and were absorbed. Agricultural wage labor started developing as early as the thirteenth century. It is said that, as early as the sixteenth century, one third of all the work done in the Netherlands (not just in agriculture) was done in the form of free contractual labor for wages and salaries. Polarization and proletarianization undoubtedly took place, and inequality in income and wealth grew. Around 1550, 50 percent of the agricultural population belonged to the land-poor and landless lower class. But the formation of an agricultural big-business class was prevented, owing to government regulations protecting the peasantry, among other reasons. Agricultural production in the region experienced uncommon growth, and with it the prosperity of the Netherlands.[12]

Developments in England proceeded similarly: weak feudal traditions and early integration of agricultural production into markets, though less with specialized high-quality products as in the Netherlands and more by way of exporting wool. In the sixteenth and seventeenth centuries, England lagged behind the Netherlands in terms of productivity and wealth, but on one important point it increasingly outpaced the Netherlands: from the fifteenth to the eighteenth century, English agriculture experienced a distinct increase in the concentration of property at the expense of small operations or tiny plots of land that were on the decline and often got absorbed. Here privatization of common land, in the form of so-called enclosures, played a much-discussed role. The privatization of common land and land consolidation by combining small properties was often implemented with the aid of parliamentary decisions that, influenced by elites from the aristocracy and gentry, served not the cause of peasant protection but instead favored the formation of large-scale agrarian capitalism. This resulted in a massive expansion of agricultural wage work and the "release" of rural laborers, who migrated to the cities, where they later helped to provide industrialization with a workforce. Between the sixteenth and eighteenth centuries, large-scale agrarian capitalism on the basis of property concentration, tenancy, and free wage labor was fully formed. This restructuring appreciably sharpened social inequality in the countryside. At the same time, it was associated with fundamental improvements in cultivation methods. The secular rise in prices for agricultural goods, which was also associated with rapid population growth, stimulated both landowners and tenants to make investments, and also to clear and purchase land, drain fens and moors, and build roads. Grazing grew in importance, and with it systematic animal husbandry. Crop rotation was fully implemented. In place of traditional peasant self-sufficiency, profit orientation and a search for renovation now became the rule for landowners and tenants, while many wage workers were ready to perform more services for higher wages. This has been called an *agricultural revolution*. In spite of rising domestic demand, England advanced to become an agrarian export country around 1650. As late as 1850, when the other European countries had already begun to catch up, the performance of English agriculture was still way ahead of the others. "Measured in terms of the number of calories per worker, productivity levels in England were twice as high as in France and three times that of the other three regions" (i.e., "Germany, Sweden and the European part of Russia").[13]

Manufacturing in Europe was also traditionally organized in a way that was far from capitalistic. It was organized partly within the framework of a household economy for home consumption (e.g., making fabrics and clothing), partly as an ancillary trade where money was earned alongside a main occupation in agriculture (this is how it remained for a long time in northern, eastern, and southeastern Europe), partly as a paid service occasionally performed in the house of the customer (as in wage work or among day laborers), but above all as independent artisanal craft production. In an artisan's workshop, goods were produced for sale, but basically either on order from the customer or as stock, so they could be sold in markets in the immediate vicinity of the artisan or else from the artisan's own little store, but not for circulation on impersonal markets with merchants acting as middlemen. Craft production rested on the combination of work and property in one and the same person, meaning that the owner worked for himself with his own hands, assisted if need be by a few helpers (journeymen and apprentices), but not as an entrepreneur and employer of a larger number of employees. Traditionally, craft production was organized corporately in guilds, that is, the artisan had to belong to the guild relevant for his profession and follow its collectively determined rules. The rules rested on the principle of fraternal equality and consciousness of a collective monopoly, but not on the principle of competition; they aimed at guaranteeing an adequate sustenance for all guild members appropriate to their social station, but they were not aimed at maximizing profit; the rules were intended to see to it "that the rich not ruin the poor"; they standardized accepted labor practices in detail and set upper limits for the size a craft workshop would be allowed to reach in its specific product line; this impeded innovation and stood in the way of accumulation. Even where organized guilds with such rules were absent, prevailing notions about adequate sustenance, fair remuneration, and moral economy were widespread in medieval and early modern trade and industry, and thus in the culture of ordinary people.

To be sure, there had long been trade and industry outside craft production, for example, in early large-scale mining and in the form of large workshops or centralized manufactories. Early on there was some incorporation of craft trades, especially from the textiles sector, into supraregional trade, into the export business. The corporate tradition did not prevent economic and social differentiation. The better-situated urban artisans ranked among the respectable middle classes, while many small artisanal livelihoods figured in the massive urban and rural poverty of the preindustrial era. Guild rules applied, if at all, in the cities, but hardly at all in the country. They were frequently broken or suspended by interventions from political authorities. Their character and content varied from country to country; they faded earlier in western Europe than in the center and the east of the continent. Yet, in principle, European artisanal production, owing to its structure and culture, was clearly and fundamentally different from capitalism.[14]

This changed when merchant capital penetrated trade and industry. Starting in the fifteenth century at the latest, growing capital requirements in connection with technical innovations more or less forced the traditionally independent, mostly cooperatively organized operators of ore mining (the *Gewerken*, or shareholders in a pit) to turn increasingly to merchants who were glad to make a financial commitment but also linked this commitment to the organization of sales and greater interference in the mining operation itself. For example, entrepreneurial mining commitments in the Alps, the Carpathians, the Erzgebirge, and the Harz mountain range became an important pillar of expansion and wealth for southern German merchant capitalists, as may be gathered from the history of the House of Fugger in the sixteenth century. In this way, mining shareholders who had once been independent were turned, step by step, into wage-dependent miners.[15]

But the most important gateway for capitalism into the world of trade and industry was in the realm of "proto-industrial" cottage industry and outwork.[16] Essentially, we are dealing here with a tension-filled symbiosis between two different ways of organizing production: On the one hand, traditional forms of artisanal handicraft, mostly in the countryside and often within a family unit, were part of the mixture. And on the other hand, there was the new element of urban merchant capital, its supraregional market orientation, and its capitalist dynamism. In the course of implementing this connection between old and new

types of production, the participating merchants became
(to some extent) *Verleger* (distributors), that is, merchant
entrepreneurs with influence on what nonetheless remained decentralized production. At the same time, the
immediate producers in this transitional system retained a
certain nominal independence as artisans, cottage industry workers, or outwork laborers at home, though in fact
they became dependent on capitalists in different ways
and were close in status to wage laborers.

To a lesser extent, this proto-industry emerged out of
urban craft production when its artisans began producing
for export, like the highly skilled metalworking craftsmen
from Solingen who knew how to seize new opportunities,
or the cloth makers of Lille who had been stuck with sales
problems, both of these examples from the seventeenth
century; here it was not just merchants who were functioning as distributors but occasionally also former artisans, for
whom the guild connection was maintained for quite some
time. For the most part, however, proto-industry emerged
in the vicinity of cities, in villages, and on the land. There
merchants turning into distributors and other middlemen
took advantage of underemployment and eagerness for
work among small peasants and the sub-peasantry, and
they profited from the low wage costs associated with these
conditions. There was usually a lack of restrictive guild rules
on the land, so these did not pose an obstacle. By advancing raw materials, awarding commissions, and acquiring
the peasant workers' products for sale on the supraregional
market, the merchant-distributors created a "rural industry," especially in the textile branch. Between the sixteenth
and eighteenth centuries, to some extent earlier and to

some extent even later, proto-industry of this kind spread throughout all of Europe, above all in less fertile rural regions, such as—to pick just some German examples—in the Sudeten mountains, the Westphalian hill country, the Thuringian Forest, and quite early along the Lower Rhine as well as in Bohemia and Silesia. Centers of textile manufacturing, metal goods production, as well as decentralized mining emerged in formerly agricultural regions of northern and western England. In the southern Low Countries, in what later became Belgium, a decline in urban craft production made itself felt during the seventeenth century, while in the villages, by contrast, there was an expansion in the proto-industrial manufacture of cloth, lace, and weapons, the result of orders from distributors who frequently supplied both raw materials and patterns for the production of the goods they had ordered. Industrial production in France grew significantly in the eighteenth century, on the average 1 to 2 percent per annum, chiefly owing to rural proto-industry. There was also much production of this kind in east central Europe, but conspicuously little south of the Alps and Pyrenees.

The forms assumed by these connections between local production and supra-local capitalism varied. They extended from the domestic system (merchants restricting themselves to buying and then selling the products of rural artisans, as in the linen trade around Bielefeld), through simple "putting out," in which distributors supplied raw materials and regulated long-distances sales (as was the case for centuries in the silk industries of northern Italy, Brussels, Antwerp, Lyons, Krefeld, and Berlin), to putting out with a centralized manufacturing plant, as when the

Calver Zeughandlungscompanie in the Black Forest employed approximately 5,000 spinners, weavers, and other textile artisans to process all the stages of wool and woolen cloth production in decentralized operations, although 168 of them were directly supervised in centralized workshops (manufactories) for dying, bleaching, and printing.

The proto-industrial system embodied a piece of capitalism in a world still pre-capitalist overall. It remained in many respects quite traditional: there was no appreciable technological progress, work took place using traditional technologies, above all in a home setting, very frequently with the participation of all members of the family, often also as a side occupation in a seasonal rhythm and according to a pre-capitalist logic. This could also be seen, for example, in the way that homeworkers varied their work schedules: they worked a great deal at times when there was a slump and prices were low, in order to hold themselves above water, whereas in boom times, when they could get high prices for their products, they cut back on the work they performed, for now they could secure familial subsistence with less effort. With the expansion of the system, supervising producers and coordinating processes became harder, and the system-induced limits to innovation and growth were pronounced. The transition to a new quality of production with self-reinforcing growth was not predetermined; a seamless transition from proto-industry to actual industrialization remained the exception, even later.

On the other hand, the proto-industrial system did upend relations of production and point toward the future. It created opportunities for millions to survive and contributed to the acceleration of demographic change. The life destinies of the outwork laborers became palpably dependent on markets and their fluctuations. Lifestyles changed and became more modern: with more equality between the sexes and with new opportunities to partake in consumption, to buy groceries like sugar, tea, and tobacco, as well as to share in fashionable innovations (white instead of brown bread, throwaway pipes, pocket watches, curtains). It was in this world of market- and consumption-oriented but decentralized and close-to-home manufacture that a kind of education toward disciplined, goal-oriented, and to a certain extent rational labor took place. This was the world in which occurred what the economic historian Jan de Vries has analyzed as an "industrious revolution," and which one can see as an early modern forerunner of industrialization starting in the late eighteenth century. After all, it was also the effects and the bottlenecks of the proto-industrial textile trade to which the great inventions of the Industrial Revolution—Hargreaves's spinning jenny (1764), Arkwright's water frame (1769), and Crompton's mule (1779)—reacted, inventions that blazed the trail for the rise of the industrial factory and hence of actual industrialization. Proto-industrialization did not lead as such to the industrial capitalism of the nineteenth and twentieth centuries. But its development proves what was already evident from the plantation economy, mining, and large areas of agriculture: capitalism was also profoundly changing the world of production long before the Industrial Revolution. What is impressive, from the perspective of the history of capitalism, is the long-term character of the observable transformation, its *longue durée*.[17]

Capitalism, Culture, and Enlightenment:
Adam Smith in Context

There was some capitalist penetration into trade, finance, agriculture, and commercial manufacturing in most countries of Europe, but only in the Netherlands and in England did these developments solidify in a way that made capitalism into the dominant guiding principle—in the Netherlands, in what were initially the provinces fighting for independence from Spain and then, following the Union of Utrecht in 1579 and Peace of Westphalia in 1648, the independent republic in the northern part of the Low Countries, and in England, a parliamentary monarchy after 1688–1689, and following the Act of Union with Scotland in 1707, the United Kingdom or Great Britain. With respect to the Netherlands and England, we may speak of a fully developed capitalist way of doing business that had powerful social and cultural impact as early as the seventeenth and eighteen centuries, even if these two economies exhibited important differences.[18] The Netherlands developed this kind of economy earlier and was *the* model for all of Europe's modernizers in the seventeenth century, but in the eighteenth century it was overtaken by the United Kingdom, which used its superior military power, but which was also developing the more sustainable basic pattern for the future: while the Dutch remained fixated on their special strengths in finance and merchant capitalism, along with exports and international financial transactions, the English also propelled capitalism forward in manufacturing and lent greater support to their economy's growth by bolstering domestic demand more than the Dutch.

Agrarian capitalism was what both countries were developing, even if with different structures. The lead these two
countries enjoyed vis-à-vis the rest of the continent could
also be seen in their advanced urbanization.[19] Among the
factors that explain this northwestern European lead, three
are most important and, moreover, are connected with
each other and with both countries' geographical position
as coastal or island nations: the huge importance of long-
distance trade as early as the Middle Ages (especially in the
case of the Netherlands), the traditional weakness of feudalism (linked in England with its history of sovereign
rule since the Norman conquest of 1066, in the Netherlands with its dynastic history), and the leading role that
both countries played in Europe's colonization of the
world since the sixteenth century.

Yet to explain the lead of northwestern Europe in the
history of capitalism, we must also point to social and cultural characteristics. A few references to England will have
to suffice. On the one hand, a mutually beneficial inter-
relationship between business and sociability cannot be
overlooked in the history of everyday life during the sixteenth and seventeenth centuries. This can be seen, for
example, in the covered arcades of the Royal Exchange in
London, where groceries as well as commercial literature
and advertising materials were on display, insurance companies and notaries offered their services, editorial staffs
were represented, and coffeehouses—there were said to be
four to five hundred in London around 1700—invited
customers to get information, consume, and be enter-
tained. Borrowing money and lending credit were widespread in everyday life, across social boundaries, and they

were linked to the market-driven expansion of consumption, including in broad segments of the population; historians have talked about a "consumer revolution" that started as early as the eighteenth century. Since the late seventeenth century, clubs and associations had mushroomed, and societies organized, to promote convivial gatherings, initiate labor disputes, provide mutual insurance, hold discussions, and play games. If one takes a closer look, one sees how market relationships, while certainly having a lot to do with competition, contest, and the pursuit of individual advantage, are also capable of eliciting trust and promoting socialization.

On the other hand, it needs to be observed that there was an increase in reading skills, especially among the urban population, and a growing dissemination of newspapers, books, and listings of all kinds. Scientific innovations were also made public in this fashion (for example, by way of meetings between scientists and practitioners in relevant organizations and associations), even if confined to rather small circles. Useful knowledge was highly esteemed, and it became a subject for professional communicators who earned a living by disseminating it.

Visitors from the continent were struck by the entertainment needs and gaming enthusiasm of the English, also by their craving for whatever was new. Even in the eighteenth century, games of chance and sports were commercial operations, and a passion for betting was paired with an inclination to calculating probabilities coolly. There were many different occasions for such gambling: at horse races, cricket matches, cockfights, or at lotteries and on the stock exchange. The culture and entertainment industries experienced an upswing. It is noteworthy how positive was the language of major Enlightenment figures when they discussed games, speculation, and entertainment: these were all seen as conditions conducive to civil society and its virtues. This was no plutocratic society, and a certain contempt for money was readily flaunted at court or in the better social circles, with all their aristocratic coloring. Class differences were pronounced and became stronger: what coffee houses were for some, brandy houses were for others. Gentlemen's clubs cut themselves off from the crowd, while workers began to form their own friendly societies. The culture of ordinary people in the country tended to be oriented more toward habits and notions of "fairness," less to profit and progress, even if rural folk were already influenced by market relations as well. But the examples cited here show that the social culture of English cities in the seventeenth and eighteenth century corresponded in a certain sense to the principles of the emerging capitalist economy, helped facilitate the breakthrough of these principles, and was in turn shaped by the capitalist economy.[20]

A reassessment took place in contemporary thinking. Influential intellectuals of the eighteenth century blazed the trail not only for an economic upgrade of capitalism but also for its philosophical and moral appreciation, even if they did not use the word "capitalism" but spoke instead of "trade" or a "commercial society." Well into the sixteenth and seventeenth centuries, a disposition that was either skeptical of or hostile toward capitalism was dominant in Europe's theologies, philosophies, and theories of the state. This skepticism was amplified in the republican

humanism of the Renaissance, with its reliance on the rediscovered Aristotle and its claim to defend virtues related
to public welfare against self-interest, private wealth, and
corruption. The most important root of skepticism toward
capitalism was, however, Christian moral doctrine, which,
in the name of brotherly love and virtuous selflessness,
rejected the pursuit of self-interest, the accumulation of
wealth, and especially every kind of profit-making financial transaction. To be sure, the Reformation and Counter-
Reformation brought about a "modern religiosity" that
stressed the "worldliness of faith" (Heinz Schilling) and contributed to an upgraded appreciation of work and profession. Max Weber emphasized the promotion of the capitalist spirit through a Puritan-Calvinist ethic, and there
undoubtedly were entrepreneurs, above all in minority de-
nominations (Mennonites, Quakers), to whom the argument applied.[21]

Yet the first far-reaching enhancement of capitalism's
reputation came out of the spirit of the Enlightenment.
Under the impact of their era's destructive wars, authors
like Grotius, Hobbes, Locke, and Spinoza worked at rede-
fining the virtues of civil society with a secularizing thrust
and informed by a concern with human rights, freedom,
peace, and prosperity. In 1748, in a clear withdrawal from
the old European mainstream, Montesquieu praised trade
as a civilizing force that contributed to overcoming barba-
rism, calming aggression, and refining manners. Other authors chimed in to the same tune, among them Bernard
de Mandeville and David Hume, Condorcet and Thomas
Paine—that is, English, French, and Dutch thinkers above
all. The common good, went the thrust of these argu-

ments, is actually promoted by the reasonable pursuit of self-interest. The advantage of the one need not be the disadvantage of the other. Commerce and morality were not locked into an inevitable opposition. The market helps replace the war of passions with the advocacy of interests. Commerce was said to promote such virtues as diligence and persistence, uprightness and discipline. Overall, a fundamental affirmation of society's new capitalist tendencies was starting to emerge. It was expected not only that these tendencies would increase prosperity but that they would also contribute to creating a social order that was better for human cooperation, one without arbitrary state intervention, with respect for liberty and individual responsibility as well as a capacity for resolving conflicts through compromise instead of war.[22]

The most systematic formulation of this view, at once realistic and utopian, was presented in 1776 by the Scottish Enlightenment thinker Adam Smith in his book *An Inquiry into the Nature and Causes of the Wealth of Nations*. Not only did Smith present an astute analysis of the key elements in capitalist economic activity—the division of labor, trade, capital formation, supply and demand, price mechanisms, and (quite centrally) the capacity to defer short-term reward with a view toward long-term utility— he also praised the enhanced personal liberty that went hand in hand with exchange transactions (including the exchange of labor power for wages), in contrast to the oppressive personal dependency that he knew came with slaveholding, serfdom, and traditional domestic service and that he rejected. By no means did he opt one-sidedly for "laissez-faire," no matter how much allowance he made for self-interest and the decisions of individual market players; rather, he also assigned the state and civil society important functions, without which, as he knew, a market economy could not function. He was far from sketching a picture of human nature as a one-dimensional *homo oeconomicus*. To be sure, he counted on human self-interest as a reliable foundation for action. But he was a moral philosopher as well as an economist. He pleaded for the view that individuals' self-love should not be restrained but rather given a direction that could contribute to promoting the common good. This pointing the way, however, could not be left to the market alone; instead, it required public morality and wisely designed institutions, especially ones providing for an appropriate regulation of the relationship linking government, society, and market. Smith criticized much about British economic policy in his time, especially its foreign economic policy, which was still mercantilist and reliant on monopolies. The "commercial society" he described was a goal to be attained in the future. He was a reformer. But he found himself in agreement with most of the trends that have been described in this chapter as the expansion and rise of capitalism, especially in England.[23]

The interpretation of emerging capitalism offered by Smith and other Enlightenment figures of the eighteenth century, as a path to greater prosperity and greater social progress, blanked out some of capitalism's weaknesses or ascribed them to institutions still in need of reform. For example, the relationship between violence and business in the world outside Europe was attributed to mercantilism. The Enlightenment reading of capitalism overlooked the elements of force that played an important role in its implementation, as in the privatization of common land and the concomitant loss of a livelihood experienced by sections of the rural population. Wherever there was a massive assertion of capitalism, even in that era, social inequality increased, even if living standards overall also rose. The fruits of growing prosperity that Smith describes were very unequally distributed.[24] Smith knew this but did not grant this finding a high priority in his thinking on the matter.

On the other hand, Smith did present an impressive draft for an economic order that fit in with a society of reasonable individuals as imagined by Condorcet and other Enlightenment thinkers. He was convinced that single individuals could best evaluate their interests for themselves. He believed that there can be a reasonable order without patronizing from an authoritarian state. He mistrusted, on the basis of past centuries' experiences, the wisdom of governing authorities and the soundness of tradition. Smith and the Enlightenment-influenced literature of his time reflected what empirical findings also confirm: capitalism was not just something lorded over or imposed on the reluctant masses by a narrow set of elites. It was also a system that—as a practical critique of old injustices, as a promise of just reward for successful effort, and as a creator of prosperity in league with liberty—could prove attractive not only for merchants and entrepreneurs but also for intellectuals and, presumably, for many "normal people" as well.

In hindsight it becomes clear that this view was not unfounded: the Netherlands and England were the two countries in the late eighteenth century that came closest to Smith's ideal of a "commercial society" or—in the language employed in this book—more capitalistic than all the other countries in Europe. But at the same time, England and the Netherlands were the most prosperous countries, and certainly also the freest, in Europe. In spite of the observable increase of social inequality in the course of implementing capitalism, the associated gains in prosperity were large enough to guarantee that the earnings of workers between 1500 and 1800 in London and Amsterdam trended upward nominally, although roughly stagnating in real terms. Meanwhile, on the continent, for example in Vienna and Florence, wages more or less stagnated nominally, while falling in real terms. Through 1800, the East-West disparity in wealth between the northwestern edge of Europe (especially England) and the biggest sections of the continent was forcefully revealed, whereas this gap had barely existed around 1500.[25] That meant a lot, and not just for elites, but also for the broad majority of the population. Whereas the destructive force of supply crises ("pauperism") was on the rise in the central part of Europe well into the "hungry" 1840s, these crises did not affect England, or if they did, it was in a way that was very much on the decline. Overcoming the Malthusian trap—at the beginning of the nineteenth century, the economist Thomas Robert Malthus predicted that population would grow faster than the available food supply if there was no deliberate population policy to brake this trend—had already succeeded in England around 1800. In large parts of Europe, this did not succeed in happening until industrialization, several decades later. For hundreds of thousands, it was now a matter of survival.

For several years now, in connection with the challenging theses advanced by the economic historian Kenneth Pomeranz in his book *The Great Divergence*, there has been an intensive discussion about why it was northwestern Europe, but not the similarly highly developed economic territory of eastern China, that succeeded in making the historic breakthrough to accelerated, ever-renewing, and self-driven growth.

The debate has not been conducted with regard to "capitalism," nor is making a contribution to that debate one of this book's immediate aims. Yet three observations following from the previous investigation may be in order.

1. If one wishes to explain the "Great Divergence," it is necessary to take a comparative look at *connections* between economy, society, state, and culture in sorting out the explanatory factors, even if this is primarily a matter of explaining differences in productivity and growth. There is a complex reality that requires looking beyond purely economic history, and here the concept of capitalism can be helpful.

2. Intra-European comparison reveals that the lead England and, with some qualifications, the Netherlands enjoyed in the late eighteenth century was the result of *long-term* processes that extended across centuries. To explain Sino-European differences, too, it would appear to be essential to look in the direction of slow changes across a long time frame.

3. Finally, a very important factor practically forc-
   ing itself on our attention is the active role
   played by governments, colonization, and proto-
   industrialization. These three factors were absent
   in China or appeared in a distinctly different
   form.[26]

At our current state of knowledge, it is evident that, around
1800, capitalism in a form going beyond merchant capitalism and with systemic force was a European phenomenon, yet fully expressed only in northwestern Europe,
however much it had been simultaneously facilitated and
codetermined by global linkages.

4

The Capitalist Era

Just as unlikely as it was that the Age of Enlightenment's optimism about progress could be sustained, equally slim were the chances that interpreting capitalism as the core of a civilizing mission might outlast that era. This buoyant interpretation sprang from the soil of preindustrial capitalism but did not survive the rise of industrial capitalism in the nineteenth century. At the beginning of the twentieth century, intellectuals like Werner Sombart and Max Weber were indeed convinced of capitalism's superior economic rationality, but they did not see it as a driving force behind moral advancement and progress in civilization. On the contrary, liberals like Weber feared the capitalist system's growing tendency to become compulsive and meaningless, and that the system might be imperiling freedom, spontaneity, and humanity in the fullest sense. Conservatives and leftists alike feared capitalism as an unstoppable erosive force replacing traditional morals with contracts, community with society, and social ties with market calculation. The socialist critique castigated exploitation, alienation, and injustice in capitalism while predicting its collapse from internal contradictions. Today attitudes toward capitalism fluctuate between acceptance and severe criticism. Many regard it as unfit to meet the challenges of the future. The idea of capitalism as a utopia appears obsolete, at least in Europe. One aim of this chapter is to understand this reversal and provide perspectives for its assessment.

The Contours of Industrialization and Globalization since 1800

To be sure, developments that had started in the preceding centuries continued, to some extent, between 1800 und 2000. *Agrarian capitalism* conquered new regions as the feudal order was eliminated step by step, which happened almost everywhere on the European continent during the nineteenth century. In the twentieth century, agrarian capitalism grew into "agribusiness" on a global scale. With growing urbanization and innovations that revolutionized commerce, transportation, and communications, *merchant capitalism* gained enormously in importance during the nineteenth and twentieth century; the dynamic growth of mass consumption, especially in the twentieth century, opened up new and highly profitable opportunities that changed the lives of many, from department and discount stores to the great retail concerns and chains of the present. Little could be accomplished without *finance capitalism*, already established by the eighteenth century but now expanding and increasingly differentiated, initially with banks, stock exchanges, and insurance companies as the most important institutions, later with investment companies and mutual funds; in the late twentieth and early twenty-first centuries, finance capitalism underwent an exorbitant expansion, without which the international financial and economic crisis of 2008 would presumably have been avoided. But what was truly revolutionary and novel after 1800 was *industrialization*, a process that, among other things, profoundly altered capitalism. As industrial capitalism, it took on a new quality.

Industrialization refers to a complex and far-reaching socioeconomic transformation process at the core of which stood three interlocking developments: first of all, innovations in technology and organization, from the development of the steam engine and mechanization of spinning and weaving in the eighteenth century to the digitalization of production and communications in the late twentieth and early twenty-first centuries; second, the massive exploitation of new energy sources (initially coal, later electricity from different sources, then oil, atomic energy, and renewable energies) that has fundamentally changed and endangered the relationship of humankind to nature; third, the spread of the factory as a manufacturing plant that, in contrast to the old putting-out system, was centralized, and in contrast to a craft workshop, used motors and machine tools and made a clear distinction between management and execution. The site of this ever-accelerating innovation process was, first of all, the sphere of industrial production, yet it soon also influenced agriculture (new cultivation methods, fertilization, mechanization) and transportation (application of new forms of energy and machines in new types of locomotion, from the railroad and steamship to air traffic and today's interdependent transportation systems), communications (from the mid-nineteenth century telegraphs to the Internet and new media), and with some delay also different administrative services, which soon grew disproportionately within an overall division of labor that was becoming more differentiated. All this led to an unprecedented increase in the productivity of most factors of production, including human labor, which became increasingly skilled but also more intense and disciplined. It also led to economic growth, which proceeded unevenly and fluctuated cyclically yet remained sustainable, even on a per capita basis and in spite of a burgeoning population. But most of all it led— and for the most part this happened after a precarious initial phase in which scarcity and poverty were aggravated— to a fundamental improvement of living conditions that could be seen by looking at real income gains. These improvements also showed up in significantly better material provisions that allowed the population, including the broad masses, to share in the progress of health care and longer lifespans, growing consumption, and a broader variety of everyday choices. Everywhere, industrialization and urbanization went hand in hand, and everywhere there was a decline in the share of the population devoted to agriculture. The agricultural sector now lost first place in favor of the industrial. In the second half of the twentieth century, the "tertiary" sector (especially trade and services) supplanted what had by now become a shrinking industrial sector. That lends a certain plausibility to talk of a "postindustrial" present, in some regions of the world.

Industrialization initially started to take place in the second half of the eighteenth century in England, and then, beginning in the first half or second third of the nineteenth century, in large parts of the European continent and North America, with offshoots in eastern and southern Europe. Japan was the first Asian country to industrialize, starting in the late nineteenth century. In the late twentieth century it was followed by large parts of Asia, especially Southeast Asia, and accelerating in the 1980s at rapid speed, China. Seldom do entire countries industrialize; it was always just individual regions. Depending on the time of industrialization and on economic, social, political, and cultural conditions, the processes of industrialization in these different countries and regions varied greatly from each other. Nowhere was the English model, and then that of the other early industrializers like the United States and Germany, simply adopted, no matter how much all these industrializations influenced each other by way of reciprocal observation and knowledge transfers, with strategies of imitation, avoidance, and adaptation. Although one cannot regard industrialization as the only path to prosperity, the prosperity gap between industrialized and nonindustrialized regions has grown enormously over the last two hundred years, both inside Europe and worldwide. As a rule, the only way to have made up in prosperity is some form of industrialization.[1] At core a socioeconomic transformation, industrialization has nonetheless worked its way into almost all areas of life and dramatically changed the world in a short amount of time, so that some authors have referred to industrialization as "the most fundamental transformation of human life in the history of the world recorded in written documents" (Hobsbawm) or as the "most important break in the history of mankind since the Neolithic period" (Cipolla.)[2] Industrialization has been extremely well researched. What is its connection to capitalism?

On the one hand, when industrialization began, capitalism already had a long history to look back on. Not even in its proto-industrially expanded form did merchant capitalism, which was widespread throughout the world, lead inescapably to full-fledged industrialization. There are many cases illustrating this point. Conversely, the case of the Soviet Union substantiates how it is also possible for industrialization to exist in a noncapitalist form. The concepts of capitalism and industrialization are defined by different features, and it is advisable to make a sharp distinction between the two of them.

On the other hand, preindustrial-commercial traditions of capitalism, wherever they persisted, significantly promoted the breakthrough to industrialization, wherever that happened in the nineteenth and twentieth century. In the nineteenth century, industrialization took place within capitalist structures everywhere. Alternative models of a centrally administered economy were tried out under Communist auspices between 1917 and 1991. They proved to be inferior.[3] China's rapid industrialization also began to take off only when the country's party leadership decided to loosen political controls step by step and make room for capitalist principles. There obviously was (and is) a pronounced affinity between capitalism and industrialization: for both, investments are of decisive importance. An inherent part of industrialization is the permanent search for new projects, as is constant engagement in new configurations; to this end, pointers and feedback from markets were and are irreplaceable. A decentralized structure that disperses decision-making among many different enterprises has proven indispensable. So far, any effort at industrialization expecting to be successful over the long run has presupposed capitalism.

Finally, industrialization changed capitalism:

1. Wage labor on a contractual basis turned into a mass phenomenon. This meant that, for the first time, the capitalist commodity form—embodied in the exchange of labor power for wages—was applied to human labor fully and en masse. Labor relations became capitalistic—that is, dependent on fluctuating labor markets, subjugated to strict calculation for capitalist purposes, and the object of direct supervision by the employer and manager. The class distinction inherent to capitalism thus became manifest, taking a tangible form as a conflict over power and the distribution of income, and becoming operative as the basis for social mobilization.

2. With factories, mines, and new transportation systems, with mechanization and the expansion of manufacturing plant, the accumulation of fixed capital reached a scale like nothing before. Alongside the numerically dominant small and medium-size businesses, large concerns and mergers came into being. This brought with it a rising need for precise control of profitability and led in principle—with significant qualifications in reality—to making entrepreneurial structure more systematic. Planned and hierarchical organization based on the division of labor gained ground as an element of capitalism along with, and connected to, the principle of the market.

3. Technological and organizational innovations became incomparably more important than they had been in preindustrial varieties of capitalism. There was now a faster pace of innovation. In Schumpeter's analysis, "creative destruction" has been the core component of the capitalist production method. In fact, it only got to be this way when industrial capitalism emerged. Factories replaced proto-industrial cottage industry for spinning yarn and weaving cloth. Steamship routes displaced towpaths and other traditional modes of transport on rivers and canals. Suppliers of electric lights quickly triumphed over gaslight companies. A hundred years later, the manufacturers of typewriters lost their market to the producers of word-processing computers. To be sure, such changes opened up new chances of success and earnings opportunities for enterprising men and women of business and their employees. As a rule, consumers profited. At the same time there were many losers. However, "constant revolutionizing of production, uninterrupted disturbance of all social conditions, everlasting uncertainty and agitation distinguish the bourgeois epoch from all earlier ones."[4] This contributed to the unpopularity of capitalism, and certainly to its continually renewed delegitimization, most apparent during capitalism's big, recurring crises, such as the ones that broke out in 1873, 1929, and 2008.

4. These crises usually arose out of excessive speculation and erroneous trends in the financial

sector, yet they also affected the "real economy." They imperiled not only a few speculators but also the life chances of broad sections of the population, and they could lead to profound social and political disruptions. Crises thus brought home another thing that distinguished capitalism in the age of industrialization from previous variants: namely, that it had become the economy's dominant regulatory mechanism, intensively influencing society, culture, and politics all at the same time. This was in contrast to centuries past, when capitalism had mostly led an insular existence and was embedded in noncapitalist structures and mentalities.

If capitalism in its developed form had been confined to a few regions in northwestern Europe prior to the epochal cusp of 1800, the kind of capitalism dynamized by industrialization took on global dimensions in the nineteenth century, and particularly in the twentieth. This can be seen not only, as already mentioned, by the capitalist penetration of new countries and regions, one after another, especially in East Asia. It is also demonstrated by the growing interdependence among capitalist processes across national and continental borders, that is, by the globalization of capitalism. This is not a new phenomenon as such, but rather something that could be observed in rudimentary outline for centuries, as was shown in the previous chapter. Yet from the 1860s through 1914, and again since the 1970s, but especially since 1990, there have been phases where globalization accelerated significantly. This faster pace of globalization could be discerned in the expansion of world trade, a certain convergence in commodity prices in different regions of the globe, the rapidly growing volume of worldwide financial transactions, the widespread rise of multinational enterprises, an increase in border-crossing labor migration, and the global range of crises. Globalization is not, to be sure, only an economic phenomenon; rather, it also occurs as a cross-border linkage connecting the fields of communications, politics, and culture. Yet capitalism is more than one of the important forces driving globalization; it is also a field on which globalization takes place, even if this does not always happen across the board or in a way that renders nation-states any less important than they used to be.[5]

From Ownership to Managerial Capitalism

Analytically, the capital-labor relationship is central to all variants of industrial capitalism. Historically, it varies a great deal. One of the factors determining this was the profound gestalt switch that unfolded in the structure and strategies of enterprises in the last two hundred years.

A conceptual distinction needs to be made between capitalists and entrepreneurs. The capitalist provides capital and decides in principle about where and for what it is used, assumes the risk involved (in theory, at least), and pockets the profits that arise. The central responsibility of the entrepreneur is to manage the enterprise, to that end making decisions about the enterprise's goals in detail, its position on the market, its internal structure, and also about how its workforce is employed.[6]

At the top of an enterprise in the first phase of industrialization, sometimes also called the Industrial Revolution, the roles of capitalist and entrepreneur were combined in one and the same person. He—it was usually a male person, but there were women as entrepreneurs, too—owned his enterprise and managed it. He raised capital, as a rule, from his own savings, through personal loans, more rarely by way of a bank credit, perhaps also through cooperation with a partner, and he was liable with his entire fortune. Even when the factory had become fully grown—for example, a mechanical spinning and weaving mill with one or two hundred workers—it usually remained a manageable enterprise constituted as a partnership, under the control of an owner-entrepreneur who frequently preferred seeing himself as "king of the castle" exercising sweeping authority. That the boss was simultaneously capitalist and entrepreneur had legitimating advantages for him. The entrepreneur's claim to leadership could be justified by reference to the risk ultimately born by the capitalist, the claim to profits with reference to the work of the successful entrepreneur.

During the early phases of industrialization, entrepreneurs had close ties with their social milieu almost everywhere, above all through their families. Start-up capital was frequently raised within the circle of family and relatives. The history of the Rothschild international banking house; of the Siemens brothers' close cooperation in establishing their enterprises in Berlin, London, and Petersburg; or of the role of the Brown family in the network of commercial enterprises in Great Britain and the United States (Liverpool, New York, Philadelphia, and Baltimore) illustrate, for the second third of the nineteenth century, how the cohesion of entrepreneurial families contributed to solving management problems, to creating cross-border business ties, and to networking with relevant social milieus. The family was thus both a precondition for and means to market success. Economic and cultural capital was passed on within the family: family firms often resulted from inheritance, which was also their goal. This expectation evidently motivated many owner-entrepreneurs to undertake investments that were future oriented. For the most part, these owner-entrepreneurs were energetic, coolly calculating persons ruthlessly pursuing advantage—typically men, rarely women—who knew how to outdo their competitors and exploit their workers. Yet their close family ties gave additional meaning, beyond the pure profit motive, to their efforts, to their struggle with competitors, and to their exploitation of workers. How little profit was regarded as an absolute value is demonstrated by situations in which family entrepreneurs dispensed with taking steps that might expand the firm. This was a relinquishment deliberately intended to avoid endangering family control over the business, a fate that might have threatened them if capital expansion had been resolutely undertaken by relying on a bank or by floating shares on the stock market. Still, the constraints of the market set limits to such noneconomic priorities. Whoever purposely relinquished dynamism was casually putting his business livelihood at risk. It was essential to push forward so as not to fall behind; merely securing the status quo was either not permitted by this competitive system, with its continuous innovation, or tolerated only within narrow limits.[7]

One can see, looking at the link between family and business, how capitalism was by no means substituting brand-new social institutions for old ones it had destroyed. Rather, at least during lengthy transitional periods, it amalgamated the social arrangements capitalism itself had brought forth with previously existing ones, implanting itself in older structures and only changing them over the long run. To this extent, it acted and continues to act in a manner that is not exactly revolutionary. It accommodates different social realities. This explains the variety of guises in which industrial capitalism has appeared to this day.

Close ties between family and enterprise are still frequent, especially in small and medium-size enterprises, which make up the majority of enterprises everywhere even today and are constantly being replenished with start-ups. Even in the management bodies of major companies that had been transformed long ago from their original form as partnerships, or that had been founded from the very start as joint-stock companies, the influence of owner-families, both founding and current, remained considerable, even in the second half of the twentieth century and especially in Great Britain and Japan.[8] Yet, on the whole, it was *managerial capitalism* that prevailed in the ever-growing field of large and giant enterprises, which as a rule were constituted as joint-stock companies based on stocks or shares (or as limited liability corporations of a similar kind). That means that the managerial function gradually shifted into the hands of salaried entrepreneurs ("managers") with limited liability. It also means that a certain separation of the capitalist and entrepreneurial function occurred, although there were, as mentioned, durable forms of cooperation between members of the owning family and managers. In any event, the owners of capital continue to exercise influence over basic decisions of the enterprise as stakeholders even in fully formed managerial capitalism. Germany and the United States were in the lead on the path to managerial capitalism, along with Japan in its own way. The driving forces were growth, capital requirements, and organization.

The German electrical engineering firm Siemens employed 90 people at home in Germany in 1854, 650 in 1874, nearly 4,000 in 1894, but by 1914 a good 57,000. Employment at the largest German enterprise—Krupp—reached 20,000 in 1887 and 64,000 by 1907, while the Thyssen-based corporation Vereinigte Stahlwerke (United Steelworks) had 200,000 employees by 1927, and the largest American enterprise U.S. Steel a respectable 100,000 in 1901 and 440,000 employees by 1929. In the late 1960s, the number of people working at Siemens worldwide was 270,000, compared to 30,000 workers and salaried employees at Deutsche Bank. By 2010 these numbers had jumped to 370,000 and 98,000 respectively. In the same year, the German post office Deutsche Post with 425,000 and Siemens with 405,000 employees occupied the top spots in the German rankings, yet they were only in eleventh and thirteenth place on the list of the largest enterprises worldwide, a list that was led by the retail conglomerate Walmart (with 2.1 million employees) and China National Petroleum (with 1.65 million employees). What stood behind these exorbitant increases in employment was a mixture of highly diverse events—mergers of

firms, above all, in addition to firms' internal growth—
and diverse goals: taking advantage of "economies of
scale," that is, of opportunities for sales and profits under
changing technological and marketing conditions (mass
production and mass markets), the pursuit of bigness and
thus also of wealth, prestige, and power, even if these aspirations did not always pay off in business terms. Frequently, too, this was expansion driven by defensive motives, since self-containment in the face of aggressive
competition can easily lead to a firm's downfall.

In the first phase of industrialization, even the most ex-
pensive enterprises got by with relatively modest capital,
as in German mining during the 1850s, where the order of
magnitude ranged from 1 to 2, or at most 3, million marks;
the capital for factories in other sectors, especially in the
extended textile branch, was without exception much
lower than this. But between 1887 and 1927 average capital for the hundred largest German enterprises increased
from 9.4 to 59 million marks. In 1901, U.S. Steel was capi-
talized at $1.4 billion. In 1970 Deutsche Bank's own capi-
tal resources still amounted to 1.4 billion DM, but by 2010
it was already €49 billion. In the same year, Siemens's own
capital resources amounted to €28 billion. As a rule, these
kinds of sums exceeded and still exceed the means available to individual owner-families. Financing via the capital market and, along with this, the organizational form of
the joint-stock company became obligatory.

Sometimes it is said that there was a "Second Industrial
Revolution" that happened during the last quarter of the
nineteenth century and first few decades of the twentieth,
specifically in those countries of Europe and North America

that had enjoyed a relatively early head start with the first round of industrialization. This alludes to the spectacular rise of "new industries" in electrical manufacturing, chemicals, and vehicle production; to the initial exploitation of petroleum as an energy source; and to the enormous increase in importance of technology and science in industrial production. But the designation also tries to capture the centralization of capital that took place via comprehensive combinations in the form of mergers, conglomerates, holdings, cartels, and interest associations. These mergers and alliances, which surfaced partly in reaction to the preceding cyclical downturns in the 1870s, were trying to limit or even eliminate competition. Among the driving forces were major entrepreneurs like John D. Rockefeller, architect of Standard Oil of New Jersey (starting in the 1870s), or Emil Kirdorf, the general director of the Gelsenkirchen Mining Company Inc. and architect of the 1893 Rhenish-Westphalian Coal Syndicate. Acting in supportive roles were often major banks that, in contrast to earlier practice, invested massively in industry and worked closely with individual industrial enterprises. Integration via stock ownership and mutual representation on executive committees proved to be tried and tested methods leading to a comprehensive networking of industrial and bank capital, without it being possible to say—in contrast to what is frequently assumed—that one side (either industry or banks) dominated the other. Subsequently there was an unprecedented concentration of power and wealth in the hands of a few major industrialists, especially in the United States, where Rockefeller—the richest man in the world, with a fortune worth about $330 billion (in 2008 values)—Carnegie,

Vanderbilt, Duke, Stanford, and others were already labeled by contemporaries with the critical and polemical designation "robber barons." Some of these major companies concentrated, like the British-American Tobacco Corporation founded in 1902, on cross-border business and developed multinational structures. Most of the big firms were highly integrated in functional terms and diversified by product: this means that inside a single company they combined, in whole or in part, the functions of raw material supply, production, processing, and distribution; at the same time, they produced entire ranges of different goods and services. They thus combined by organizational means what in other, earlier cases had been handled by independent enterprises that were more highly specialized and linked to each other through market ties.

As a result, there emerged highly complex, systematically structured, elaborately coordinated megastructures with managerial personnel who were, increasingly, academically certified. In the late nineteenth and early twentieth centuries, these corporate structures were vertically integrated, centralized, and rather hierarchic, after 1945 in the West more likely to be rather decentralized and structured as federations of semiautonomous units. Overall, this was a profound change of form for capitalism. What was once the clearly dominating form of coordination via market mechanisms was now, much more strongly than before, complemented by coordination using organizational and quasi-political methods. This was referred to as *organized capitalism*, although, in spite of all the alliances and monopolistic tendencies, severe competition continued to take place even between these gigantic enterprises, competitive challenges that could even threaten these firms' autonomy and existence. Relative to the many more numerous small and medium-size enterprises, the big enterprises did remain in the minority everywhere. Yet they were extremely important. In 1962 the fifty largest American industrial enterprises had over a third, and the five hundred largest together over two-thirds, of the country's commercial-industrial capital. They were, incidentally and without exception, managed by white, predominantly Protestant men from a background that was (at least) middle class and with (at least) a college degree.[9]

The rise of managerial capitalism was accompanied by great hopes and great fears. Both have, as a rule, proven to be exaggerated.

It was hoped that managerial capitalism—owing to the dispersion of ownership it made possible and to ownership's declining importance for recruiting management—would produce a bit of democratization. On the one hand, the dispersion of stock ownership, its growing attractiveness for investors both small and large, and its increasing importance for insuring against life risks and for care of the elderly did indeed significantly strengthen and broaden capitalism's anchoring in society. It has tied life for the multitude even more clearly than before to the ups and downs of capitalist business. One need only think of the widespread policies for old-age provision via pension funds that are among the biggest actors on financial markets. In addition, the criterion "ownership of the means of production" has become less important for recruiting and promoting management, and there is a difference between the typical career paths of owner-entrepreneurs and managers. Yet access to the bastions of economic power overall have hardly opened up much further. Rising from dishwasher to millionaire has remained the exception. A high degree of intergenerational status inheritance is also brought about by the selection process typical of managerial capitalism. This process, in addition to training acquired both scholastically and practically, puts a premium on the cultural capital imparted by social background and the networking relationships associated therewith.

Conversely, it was feared that the rise of managers would increase irresponsible action in the upper echelons of firms, since salaried entrepreneurs would certainly no longer be forced to answer for their failures by putting their entire economic and social livelihood on the line, just as (conversely) they would only profit personally in a limited way from any entrepreneurial success. In the light of recent experiences with "structured irresponsibility" in today's finance capitalism, it is important to understand why this fear did not, on the whole, come true during the classical era of managerial capitalism—which, in the West, lasted through the 1970s and 1980s. On the one hand, those components of managerial earnings linked to a company's success, including managers' shares in capital, contributed to managerial responsibility. On the other, this occupational group developed professional attitudes, with corresponding techniques for mutual social control. But, above all, in spite of growing mobility, success and failure, even for salaried entrepreneurs, remained quite visibly tied to the success and failure of *certain* enterprises—"their" enterprises—both for the managers themselves and for others. This proved decisive (whereas it seems to be different in today's financial market capitalism). The identification of an Emil Rathenau with "his" managerially run enterprise AEG around 1910 was certainly not much weaker than the way that the son of rival company founder Wilhelm von Siemens identified with "his" traditional enterprise, still controlled by family even after having become a joint-stock company.

As a whole, however, managers were less influenced and constrained by extra-economic (e.g., family-related) considerations than were owner-entrepreneurs. For the salaried entrepreneurs of managerial capitalism, therefore, economic motives were actually more clear-cut than they were for the owner-entrepreneurs of the Industrial Revolution. On the whole, therefore, the salaried entrepreneurs should have been able to reach decisions more dynamically and behave more expansively than owner-capitalists.[10]

Financialization

The tendency to detach economic action from social contexts, the concentration on goals of profit and growth coupled with a simultaneous indifference to other goals, the autotelic character of capitalism, a feature already inherent in managerial capitalism though not yet made absolute— over the last several decades, all these trends reached new heights with the arrival of "financialization," the rise of what can be called *financial market capitalism, finance capitalism*, or *investor capitalism*. The level attained by financialization is of a degree that has imparted a new quality to the system and has presented it with new, yet unsolved, challenges. Finance capitalism—as the epitome of business transactions that have little to do with production and exchange of goods but that are made above all with money and (in the milieu of) money changers, brokers, banks, stock exchanges, investors, and capital markets—is an old phenomenon, as was shown above. Yet since the 1970s something new has happened, in three respects:

1. What happened was connected with the end of the Bretton Woods system of international currency regulation and the drastic oil price increases of the 1970s, with the onset of deregulation, and with a certain degree of deindustrialization in some Western countries that led to a rapid expansion and upgrading of the financial sector, especially in England and the United States, where this sector's share of overall production grew from 2 percent in the 1950s to approximately 8 or 9 percent in 2008. The assets of banks grew explosively. Cross-border capital movements swelled from 4 percent of overall product worldwide in the 1980s to 13 percent in 2000 and 20 percent in 2007. Much of this was accounted for by the transfer from oil-producing and emerging market countries (China, Southeast Asia, India, Brazil) to Europe and North America. But foreign investments from the first countries to industrialize also boomed, with finance and insurance getting the lion's share. As the investor George Soros wrote in 1998: "The system is very favorable to financial capital, which is free to pick and choose where to go. . . . It can be envisaged as a gigantic circulatory system. . . . It is market fundamentalism

that has put financial capital into the driver's seat." Jürgen Stark, longtime chief economist at the European Central Bank, decreed in 2011 that the financial sector had long since left its ancillary role in service to the economy behind, that it had become too large and self-referential. The "neoliberal" policy of deregulation that started in England and the United States but soon took effect internationally contributed greatly to this trend, as it did to the exorbitant rise of profits for bankers. In order to participate in the boom of the financial sector,[11] major industrial enterprises like General Motors and General Electric added on their own financial service providers, which soon brought in higher profits than each company's core business itself. Investment banks, investment funds, over-the-counter private equity companies, and other capital investment and holding companies sprang up in large numbers. There was talk of "financialization." A large share of capital movements served (and serves), not investment for productive purposes, but rather speculation, even if the two are often hard to distinguish clearly from one another. Sizable profits were earned that did not correspond to any added value. Expectations of garnering the highest possible profits increased, along with eagerness to undertake great risks. It must be conceded that the financial sector was and is also intrinsically heterogeneous; municipal savings banks or cooperative banks remained more strongly committed to the traditional banking business. But aggressive hedge funds, acting like "locusts" (as Germany's former Social Democratic labor minister and party chair Franz Müntefering called them), bought up profitable businesses, "rationalized" them, cannibalized them, and divided them up in order to resell them at a profit and then move on. Ivan Berend writes: "The morals of solid banking, together with trust in institutions, were lost. Gambling replaced a solid business attitude and increased both gains and risks. The boom culminated in the first years of the twenty-first century." Left to itself, driven by tough competition, and largely detached from embedment in the real economy or society, at least this part of the capitalist economy proved incapable of developing and implementing generally accepted rules for conducting business.[12] The mathematicization and digitalization of speculative transactions has led to an economy in which money managers have acted not only as driving forces but increasingly also as driven entities addicted to their own techniques and ever stiffer competition.[13]

2. Credit and thus debt have characterized capitalism from the start. But in the last quarter of the twentieth and in the first decade of the twenty-first century, the inclination to indebtedness has grown exorbitantly in many countries and sectors. For example, the quotient of government debt rose, and indeed this was happening long

before the international financial crisis of 2008
led governments to renew their massive borrowing with the aim of bailing out their countries'
banks. Germany's national debt quotient (measured as a share of gross domestic product) oscillated between 16 and 24 percent from the
beginning of the 1950s through 1975, yet by
1985 it had climbed to 41 percent, by 1995 to
56 percent, and by 2005 to 69 (81 percent by
2011). The corresponding figures for France are
16 percent (1975), 31 percent (1985), 55 percent
(1995), 67 percent (2005), and 86 percent (2011).
In Sweden the quotient rose between 1975 and
2005 from 28 percent to 50 percent (with an in-
terim peak of 84 per cent in 1996), in the United
States from 33 percent to 68 percent, in Brazil
from 30 percent to 69 percent, and in Japan from
24 percent to 186 percent.[14] A second example:
the savings quotient of Americans (private households) was almost 5 percent in 1930, reached
more than 10 percent in the early 1980s, but then
fell to 0 percent by 2005–2007 (and was at 2 percent in 2013). A third example: the average equity capital of many American and European
banks before the recent crisis was less than 10 percent, frequently less than 5 percent, and sometimes not even 1 percent of their proven total
assets, compared with around 25 percent at the
beginning of the twentieth century; most of the
remainder consisted of outside capital, that is, of
"debts."[15]

Each one of these three phenomena is quite complex and has different causes: first, peculiarities of government policy, which frequently has no reliable mechanisms for self-restraint and readily postpones solutions to problems into the future; then the rapid rise of consumer capitalism since the 1950s, which solidifies acceptance of capitalism among the broad population but simultaneously stimulates an inclination to live beyond one's means by making available highly attractive sales pitches, permanent demand stimulus, and seductive offers of credit; and, finally, decision-making structures inside banks, which cause high earnings not to be reinvested but instead distributed to stockholders and managers.

Yet, at a general level, all three of the variants of indebtedness mentioned here may be understood as indicators of one and the same fundamental change, which the sociologist Ralf Dahrendorf described in 2009 as the problematic transition from "savings capitalism" to "pump capitalism." In 1979 another sociologist, Daniel Bell, had already analyzed the tension between the necessity of saving inherent to capitalism, that is, of postponing rewards into the future, and the equally system-inherent necessity of spending on consumption in the capitalist present. In the meantime, this contradiction has intensified. We are dealing with a lasting source of destabilization for capitalism in the age of its financialization, with the core of an unresolved crisis and with, on top of this, a fundamental problem of culture and politics in the relatively affluent countries of the present time.[16]

3. Power relations and decision-making processes at the higher echelons of major enterprises have also shifted over the last several years and decades, on the road from managerial to finance or investor capitalism. In managerial enterprises, which were clearly dominant among large firms through the 1980s, the executive committee, company board, or even CEO had considerable autonomy and weight vis-à-vis owners' interests, especially when business was going well. Either the bank—often closely linked with a production, trade, or service enterprise in a long-term relationship—saw to it that there was managerial autonomy, since the bank was less interested in short-term profits than it was in long-term success and therefore backed management (with credit, among other things) even in opposition to stockholder interests (especially in Germany and Japan). Or the board of the enterprise enjoyed relative independence because ownership of the company was dispersed among numerous small and medium-size stockholders who, given their fragmentation, were hardly in a position to issue a collective challenge and were content with decent returns on their investment even if the last opportunity to squeeze out increased profits was not always fully exhausted (as in the United States, above all). In both cases the chances were great that the management of the

enterprise would reinvest large portions of the profits made, rather than distribute them to owners—which strengthened management's relative autonomy vis-à-vis the capital market.

This changed with the rise of asset management companies (especially the large investment and pension funds) and of increasingly aggressive firms specializing in investment banking. They are in tough competition with each other for investors and savers, whom they promise yields on interest or shares in future profits that are favorable. Their track record can be expressed in a few key figures and is highly transparent. Even small differences count in their competition for investors and savers, whose assets they bundle together into weightier securities and whose interests as owners ("shareholder value") they promise to make their own and represent very toughly, professionally, and constantly against those of management.[17]

The logic of the capital markets now penetrates much more directly into company strategies than was the case in times when ownership or managerial capitalism was the distinctive model. The market becomes more ubiquitous and more compulsive. Room to maneuver for individual company managements is shrinking. Enterprises are becoming more like one another. The influence of the banks is declining. The representatives of the funds exercise control, but they are simultaneously controlled; they demand permanent accounting, which they must permanently render themselves. They can sell at any time and restructure their portfolios, which gives them great power. Volatility is on the rise. On average, an investor from the 1960s held his stocks (in New York) for eight to nine years, but now it is less than a year. Important decisions are made by fund directors, investment bankers, stockbrokers, analysts, and rating experts, who are managers but often speak in the name of the owners and represent their interests in obtaining high returns. They usually have no ties to the many enterprises over whose fate they help decide, so to speak, from the outside. They are not particularly interested in these enterprises' contents, traditions, and agents. They decide on the basis of usual performance indicators and sensitive market signals, and they are oriented one-dimensionally to profit or shareholder value. This is what they must do; otherwise they will damage their fund.[18]

In this relatively aloof and still, at core, deregulated system of investor capitalism, it is neither urgent nor possible to justify the very abstract activity of these "money managers" in the context of more far-reaching, perhaps noneconomic purposes. In one revealing scene from his reality-saturated novel *Bonfire of the Vanities*, Tom Wolfe depicts how the successful, prosperous investment banker and Wall Street broker Sherman McCoy attempts to explain to his inquiring six-year-old daughter what he does for a living so that she can understand and admire his job. At his beach club on Long Island, the assembled family members

await his answer with anticipation. The attempt
at explaining his job fails, the daughter breaks
into tears, and it remains for the reader to decide
if this is owing to the complexity of McCoy's line
of work or to whether his occupation really makes
no sense beyond the job itself and the goal of
enrichment.[19]

It cannot be emphasized strongly enough that
(mostly smaller, but quite numerous) owner-
run businesses, manager-capitalists of the classic
kind, and the new type of globally active finance
capitalists exist everywhere alongside each other
and in the greatest variety of overlapping forms.
Certainly, contemporary capitalism cannot be
reduced to finance, financial market, or investor
capitalism. The rise of finance and investor capitalism during the last several decades does,
however, represent a far-reaching change in the
overall system. Functional differentiation within
capitalism has advanced significantly: mobilizing
capital and investing have been separated even
more sharply from other dimensions of leading
firms. Raising and investing capital were made
the responsibility of specialized actors operating
strictly according to the logic of capital markets.
This has considerably strengthened the weight of
the capitalist function relative to the entrepreneurial and the managerial functions. More radi-
cally than ever before, fundamental investment
decisions have been detached from the contexts
in which they were once embedded. The logic of
markets has further emancipated itself from any

consideration of noneconomic interests and orientations. Furthermore, decision-making structures have clearly overstepped the boundaries within which individual enterprises operate, the outer edges of which have become more fluid. The international financial crisis of 2008 conspicuously demonstrated what self-destructive and all-around dangerous potentials lurk inside the dynamic of the new investor capitalism when this new type of capitalism is left to itself—and that means left to the banks, investors, stockbrokers, and other "money managers."[20] What is at stake is finding new forms of embedding. Whether that can be done remains an open question.

Work in Capitalism

Since Marx, Weber, and many others, "free" wage labor on a contractual basis has been regarded as the central form assumed by work in capitalism. Yet the debate about whether this is accurate and how this should be understood is once again in full swing. The move toward more global perspectives has intensified historians' awareness of how capitalist businesses could and can also flourish on the basis of unfree labor. We need only think of the colonial and postcolonial plantation economy with slave labor and other forms of forced labor, of the exploitation of prisoners and inmates of camps in the wars and dictatorships of the twentieth century, but also of new forms of unfree labor today, especially in the global South. Historians have, moreover, become more intensely aware of how forms of bound labor

and extra-economic compulsion have also played a major
role for a long time in European and North American agrarian and industrial capitalism, as is demonstrated by the history of serfdom and farm servants, but also of peonage and
"indentured laborers." Is not the very distinction between
unfree labor and free labor on a contractual basis altogether
quite permeable and blurry in light of the many elements
of unfreedom in the reality of wage work? Should one not
draw the logical conclusion and expand the usual definitions of the "working class" so that all types of subaltern
persons or families—and not just wage workers and the
members of their families—are included?[21] In this book,
nevertheless, I hold to the notion of wage labor as the central form of work in capitalism for these reasons:

1. For one thing, the trend toward comprehensive
   commodification represents a key component of
   the capitalist system, and wage labor is the most
   consistent application of this principle to human
   labor (although not the only one).
2. For another, in spite of numerous exceptions and
   countervailing tendencies, *in the long run* wage
   labor has become and is becoming more extensive
   and widespread, and not just in the course of capitalist industrialization in the West but (in the
   meantime) worldwide. As capitalism, industrial
   capitalism in particular, has widened and deep-
   ened, wage labor became, and is still becoming,
   step by step, the prevailing form of work, although it appears in many forms and combinations. This had, and still has, something to do
   with the fact that free wage labor on a contractual

basis corresponds best, in principle, to the particular kind of instrumental rationality inherent in capitalist enterprises. For, unlike workers who perform bonded labor with their entire person over long periods of time (such as slaves), wage workers who are contractually obligated to perform certain services temporarily but are otherwise free as well as terminable—wage workers like this allow businesses and employers to recruit, shift, and if need be also quickly dismiss employees with a view toward entrepreneurial objectives. This is advantageous to the company's interest. Under conditions of developed, differentiated labor markets, and in the face of rapid economic change as capitalist normality, it was and is in the interest of capitalist actors to prefer wage labor to unfree labor.

3. Finally, it should be taken into consideration that an employment relationship under wage labor can be terminated by the worker as well as by the employer. The employment relationship may subjugate the worker's labor power, but not his or her entire person, to the employer's order-giving authority and the constraints of the enterprise. This is an important and coveted element of freedom. The transition to wage work could and can have a liberating effect, even though entry into such an exchange relationship of work for wages is frequently a matter of urgency for the worker on sheer grounds of survival, and although the employment relationship, once accepted, is usually characterized by much control and discipline.

This social and legal quality distinguished and still distinguishes wage labor, in principle, from the different forms of unfree labor, and this distinction needs to be taken seriously from the standpoint of life histories and historiography.[22]

Yet, on the other hand, it bears repeating one more time that, under certain conditions, capitalism has functioned and can continue to do so on the basis of unfree labor, and that, again under certain conditions, capitalist agents have sometimes preferred and continue to prefer exploiting unfree labor. They preferred and prefer whatever, under given conditions, promises higher and sustainable profits. And above all it needs to be emphasized that, in the long history of capitalism, free wage labor has mostly not appeared in any pure form, but rather in amalgamation with other forms of employment.

In an elementary sense, and to a limited extent, wage labor existed prior to capitalism. Certainly, before capitalism the largest share of dependent labor was performed under conditions of bondage—as slave labor or (as in medieval and early modern Europe) by serfs and peasant underlings, by servants and maids in servile status, and by journeymen dependent on masters and guilds. Nonetheless, over the centuries, there were numerous persons with either few or no possessions—men, women, and children— who performed work for remuneration, usually for short periods and constantly changing jobs, often also at different sites, for lords and peasants, for artisans and merchants, in parishes and monasteries, at construction sites or in workshops: they were employed as agricultural workers with different designations, as day laborers, casual laborers, seasonal or migratory workers, as temporary workers of many different kinds. One barely made a living this way, and yet the payments in kind or money wages achieved this way frequently supplemented the small incomes that the individual or his family drew at the same time from other sources, for example, from the ownership of tiny properties. In one and the same family, at one and the same place of work, there were often persons with different occupational status working together, as in early modern plantations where slaves, "indentured laborers" obligated to work for a time, and free wage workers coexisted. With the penetration of capitalism into agriculture and cottage industry, there was an increase in the number of wage workers above all on the land. Through the gradual loosening of traditional ties (e.g., of the journeyman's dependence on his master and his master's guild) and the growing inclusion of working people such as artisans and cottage workers in supraregional market relationships, moreover, capitalism reinforced the elements of wage labor inside traditional employment relationships. With respect to dependent laborers, too, it was the case that social relationships shaped by capitalism seldom made their appearance abruptly and by quickly destroying old ways; instead, they ensconced themselves in traditional social relationships, expanding, loosening, and relativizing them (under the impact, to be sure, of tensions and conflicts), changing them step by step. One and the same person might, in the course of his life, occupy many different positions, and these often included distinctive phases of underemployment and unemployment, and certainly also of dire poverty.[23]

It will be evident that this hodgepodge of wage labor marked by countless transitions and mixed forms cannot be neatly subdivided and is therefore very difficult to quantify. And yet, if one employs a generous conception of "proletarian" that includes day laborers and casual laborers, agricultural workers and homeworkers, workers in manufactories and mines as well as servants and journeymen, then one can concur with Charles Tilly's estimate that in 1550 about one-quarter and in 1750 almost 60 percent of Europe's population should be included in the proletarian classes. More than half of these lived on the land. It was therefore not some idyllic world, clearly ordered or even static, that was then transformed by nineteenth-century industrial capitalism. Instead, this was a world in motion, with little in the way of formalized employment relationships and living conditions, a world replete with scarcity, destitution, and distress—at least in the large and rapidly growing sector of society underneath the rural and urban middle classes.[24]

Yet only in the nineteenth and twentieth centuries did fully developed wage labor start to become an overwhelming mass phenomenon, especially in the West, although there were rudiments of modern wage labor in other parts of the world as well. One thing that helped in the West— something partly accomplished by revolution and war (as in France, the United States, and Haiti), though more often because of reforms (incremental changes that usually dragged on for decades)—was the abolition of those traditional social orders in which unfree labor had become stabilized. The list of changes favoring wage labor would have to include the prohibition of the slave trade (starting in

1808), followed by the ban on slavery itself, but also the judicially enforced outlawing (starting in the 1820s in the United States) of "indentured" servitude, that form of temporary bondage in which workers were contractually bound to work off a debt for transport costs paid in advance (for example, to cover a journey across the Atlantic). Also on the list would be the emancipation of the peasantry and the abolition of serfdom (which finally happened in Russia after 1861), along with the abolition or dilution of guild regulations in the course of implementing "freedom of trade." Against this background, what happened in most countries was a quite gradual advancement of wage labor going hand in hand with the gradual implementation of capitalistic principles, often through mixed forms of work that persisted for a long time.

The "temporary servitude" of "indentured laborers" (contract workers) represented such a mixed form; it was a category that included the important group of "coolies," half-free laborers from Asia who were transported across long distances in order to be employed in the plantations (sugar, rubber, tobacco, etc.) that underwent renewed expansion after 1860, mostly in tropical and subtropical regions of Asia, America, and Africa. Another example would be the slaves for hire who were rented out by their owners to entrepreneurs in the southern states of the United States, Latin America, and West Africa and who did temporary work for wages, some of which they had to pass on from their temporary employers to their permanent owners. Russian serfs were also employed from time to time as wage workers, on assignment from their masters. In the South African diamond mines during the nineteenth century, "closed compounds" were set up in which miners were locked up under prisonlike conditions: an example of mixing wage and forced labor. One must certainly recall the millions of homeworkers in the European putting-out system, who basically performed wage work but still did this in the form of traditional outwork, within the family unit and inside their own four walls. This usually happened in the countryside, although after 1870 more and more in the big cities, too, where clothing and other ready-made apparel would be manufactured in home industries, as a rule by women and children under the heavy supervision of intermediate entrepreneurs and under oppressive working conditions: the sweatshops of New York, Paris and Berlin around 1900 come to mind. In Prussia and other German states, a legally codified servile status (Gesinderecht) lasted until 1918, a status that curtailed liberties for large categories of agricultural workers and household servants; nonetheless, farmhands, maids, and domestic servants gradually became wage laborers of a special kind. There were other relationships of mixed employment in which wage labor appeared as one element among many. In the long run, however, the wage labor element prevailed.[25]

In addition to the gigantic construction sites of the time, it was above all in and by way of industrial factories and mining that wage labor became a mass phenomenon. This was not only because this sector grew disproportionately large during the first phases of industrialization, because workers appeared here in huge crowds, and because this was also a field where small and large enterprises were active, an area in which the transition from ownership to

managerial capitalism as described above was notably taking place. More to the point, it also had to do with the
structure of industrial enterprises and their relationship to
their social environment. In factories and mines, wage
labor was taking place at sites spatially separated from the
households of those working there. Moreover, these were
enterprises with a division of labor, a separation of management and execution, work sequences that were becoming more instrumentally rational, and with corresponding
requirements of discipline. This included adjustment to
specific structures of time and meant that, more clearly
than before, the sphere of labor was divorced from other
areas of life, spatially and temporally. Its capitalist logic
could unfold relatively independently in that distinct industrial sphere. Here wage labor developed in a fairly pure
form. It was experienced as such. Indeed, workers encoun-
tered wage labor as something that united them a bit beyond their specialization and distinguished them from
management. A worker might come across instances of cooperation between capital and labor but also times when
the relationship was fraught with conflicts and tensions.
These conflicts revolved in part around questions about
how to distribute the product being made (e.g., in the
conflict over wages and work time); they also concerned
questions of power, of who had precedence or would be
subordinated, for example in controversies about the organization of work or about autonomy and, later on,
codetermination.

Of course, industrial work had precursors in the less numerous early modern manufactories and mines. But in all

these respects, "big industry" in the form of textile factories, coal mines, steelworks, and mechanical engineering
companies was something new in the era of industrialization, separated from what people had been accustomed to
by a certain hiatus with respect to time, space, and experienced structures. Accordingly, it captured the imagination
of contemporaries, who were both fascinated and shocked
by it. "Big industry" had shaped the emerging discussion
about "capitalism" since the middle of the nineteenth century. This industrial capitalism also shaped the concepts
and views of Marx.[26] In the first phase of industrialization,
workers suffered poverty and deprivation under the harsh-
est kind of exploitation, enduring extremely long working
hours and low wages, and being subject to sharp discipline, both inside and outside industrial factories. The
children laboring in mine shafts, the long, uniform rows
of young women lined up next to their mechanized work
stations in huge textile mills, the living quarters in dark
cellars of overcrowded tenements in the working-class sections of the rapidly growing city, the desperate uprising of
starving outworkers facing pressure from more productive
industrial factories, like the Silesian weavers in the 1840s
whose plight was later on dramatized by the popular poet
Gerhart Hauptmann on the stage—these are pictures of
misery and capitalist exploitation that have been engraved
in collective memory.

These constellations cannot be explored in detail here,
any more than it is possible to describe every aspect of the
gradual upward trend (though a trend frequently interrupted by crises and wars) of improved working and living

conditions that took place in large parts of the world in spite of lingering and newly emerging pockets of exploitation and poverty that accompanied the ongoing process of industrialization. After countless tribulations and conflicts, innovations and reforms in the world of work as well as in politics and society, the character of wage labor has profoundly changed. In a large core sector dominated by large private firms and public enterprises, the practices implemented extensively by the third quarter of the twentieth century were earnings increases geared toward the family wage, forceful reduction in working hours (even if accompanied by equally forceful intensification of work), hedging against risk by guaranteed entitlements in case of accident, sickness, old age, and dismissal, as well as individual and collective labor rights. This is true, at least, for large portions of the industrialized world. The applicable term is "standard employment"—"normal working conditions" (*Normalarbeitsverhältnis* in German)—but this makes it easy to forget that, for centuries, this achievement was anything but standard or normal, that even today it represents an exception, and that it is called into question by new developments even in places where it had already been implemented.[27] Here is a brief list of the three most important motors driving those developments that somewhat helped achieve such "normal working conditions." All three are fundamentally connected with wage labor.

1. In businesses, advances in productivity were achieved that first made the above-mentioned

improvements possible. In the interest of increasing productivity, numerous business managements at an advanced stage of industrialization discovered that shortening working hours, careful treatment of "labor power" as a resource, and certain concessions to workers' demands also served business success. These changes were favored not only by philanthropically- and reform-minded entrepreneurs, like Robert Owen in Scotland or Ernst Abbe in Jena, who were always around. There were also soberly calculating managers and owners of capital who became, to some extent, reformers within their own businesses, especially in branches that made high demands on the skills of their personnel.

2. Yet that would not have been enough to initiate change. Equally important, therefore, was a second impetus: government intervention. The readiness of state institutions to use laws, ordinances, and controls in order to combat abuses in the working world and secure rights for workers had many motives. One such motive, however, was connected to the public visibility that wage labor gained when it no longer took place at home, on a peasant's holding, or in some other traditional relationship, but rather at a separate site, in the factory or coal mine. This was the case, for example, with child labor. It once had been regarded as a normal part of any agricultural operation or of proto-industrial cottage

work. But now that it was detached from the family and the household, it became a problem to be monitored and subjected to critical scrutiny, especially by a public concerned about education: this scrutiny made an important contribution by politicizing the problem and getting the state to actively fight child labor. For example, in Prussia after 1839, a ban implemented in several stages contributed decisively to the eventual disappearance of industrial child labor in mines and in factories.[28] The next section of this chapter examines the role of state interventions in capitalism.

3. Finally, a word about the labor movement. Wage labor is, in key respects, not free at all. Not freedom, but subordination and discipline are what the wage labor relationship entails for workers after they have entered into it. One may, moreover, regard it as frivolous or cynical to regard nonownership of the means of production as proof of "freedom," as sometimes happens. But wage workers are indeed free—unlike forced laborers, slaves, serfs, indentured laborers, servants, farmhands in servile positions, and artisan journeymen embedded in corporative rules—to the extent that they enter an employment relationship that is, in principle, free of extra-economic compulsion, that they can decide to terminate of their own free will, and that involves the labor services of the worker but not the subordination of him or her as a whole

person. This is the emancipatory element of wage labor, in contrast to the varieties of bonded labor that were once dominant. One should not lose sight of this emancipatory element even when correctly emphasizing the asymmetry built into the employer-employee relationship, when clarifying how "free" and "unfree" labor have differed from each other more gradually than in principle with respect to many of their everyday effects, and when appreciating how freedom from extra-economic compulsion only gradually prevailed in the course of capitalist industrialization and how, as is well known, this freedom was repeatedly rolled back by the massive use of forced labor in the wars and dictatorships of the twentieth century.

An immediate expression of wage laborers' freedom was and is their ability, individually and collectively, either to defend themselves or— much more frequently—to formulate and enforce claims to improvements in working conditions. Only in capitalism could autonomous labor movements become strong, and only in the industrial capitalism of the nineteenth century did this happen in an era when wage labor became a mass phenomenon inside (but also outside) the factory.

The energy of the labor movement was ignited, to put the point in systematic terms, by three challenges: First, labor movements grew out of efforts to protect against the kinds of insecurity that routinely increased when the capitalist way of doing business took hold. Welfare funds, cooperatives, and friendly societies come to mind. Second, the labor movement grew out of the above-mentioned conflicts over distribution and authority that are inherent in the capital-labor relationship; this was manifested by spontaneous and organized protests, above all by strikes. Finally, though, labor movements gained and continue to gain their energy from defending traditional, noncapitalist forms of work and living against an ever more pervasive capitalism, as when the principles of a traditional culture embodied in a "moral economy" (with its emphasis on the "just price") were defended against the capitalist logic of individualization, competition, changing prices, and growth.[29] In altered form, this thrust has had a long life, basically lasting through the present time, as in the struggle for a minimum wage today: it has taken the form of defending or demanding work that is just and humane, as opposed to the routinization, degradation, instrumentalization, and commodification of work under capitalism, a cause classically formulated in Karl Marx's critique of alienation.

This resulted in the development of what was certainly Europe's most important movement of protest and emancipation in the nineteenth and early twentieth centuries, a movement that contributed mightily to the democratization of politics and society, even if during the twentieth

century it split into an (internally diverse) social
democratic branch and a Communist-totalitarian
branch that has since become discredited. It was
the pressure of workers' demands on the shop
floor, during strikes, by trade unions, and in politics that contributed to the aforementioned improvements in working conditions and thus, one
might say, to civilizing capitalism.

Historical comparison makes it clear that labor
movements of this kind were not the inevitable
outcome of the tension between capital and labor.
Instead, underlying the growth of labor movements was a long series of cultural and political
preconditions that existed to a great degree in
large parts of the West in the nineteenth and
early twentieth centuries. These same prerequi-
sites have not survived at the same level of
strength until the present day, nor can they necessarily be found in other regions of the world.
For example, Chinese wage workers today certainly experience commodification, capitalist instrumentalization, uprooting, and exploitation in
a manner that is roughly comparable with what
European workers suffered during the first phase
of industrialization, even if the Chinese experience has been compressed into a shorter time,
making it especially disruptive. Chinese wage
workers also protest and rebel, in large numbers,
almost daily. Yet in a People's Republic that continues to be partially dictatorial, Chinese workers'
actions, without exception local events—protests

and petitions at the workplace, strikes boycotts, blockades, sit-ins—have so far not coalesced to become a supra-local, supraregional protest and emancipation movement.[30]

Two developments in the history of wage labor whose future is hard to predict merit special mention. For one, in a trend parallel to the financialization of capitalism, and as a consequence of changes in technology and market organization, there has been a discernible fragmentation of work, including of wage labor, in space and time. Whereas in the Federal Republic of Germany in 1970, the ratio between workers in fulltime employment and all others in the workforce doing part-time and short-time work or are temporarily and marginally employed—in other words, workers in so-called atypical employment conditions—was 5:1, this shifted by 1990 to 4:1 and 2:1 by 2013. Every third person in 2013, then, was working either part time, temporarily, on subcontract, or in a mini-job. The elasticity of gainful employment and the fluidity of working conditions are on the rise. Demands on the individual's flexibility are increasing. The workplace is losing the clear contours that it first acquired in the nineteenth century. The new communications media are facilitating new forms of outwork. A new regime of time is emerging in the gray areas between working time and free time, with part-time work and flex-time bringing fresh opportunities as well as new dependencies and risks. The findings need to be assessed in a differentiated way. Not every employment relationship that is "atypical" in this sense is precarious, especially not every part-time employment. Undoubtedly, this fluidity also harbors new opportunities, for example, to link earning a living with other activities, to connect work with leisure, and to reconcile professional with family life. On the other hand, there is the danger that making employment conditions more flexible and work more fragmented will lead to a perilous erosion of individual identities and of social cohesion, to the extent that these fixtures of modern life depend on continuous work of the kind that has been the case in the "work societies" of the West ever since the nineteenth century. In any event, the binding force of work, its power to shape structures of social welfare, create cultural ties, and socialize individuals, seems to have diminished recently.[31]

Finally, it is worth looking at capitalism and wage labor in the regions of the "global South" that industrialized thoroughly only in the last several decades: wage labor there, which is extremely diverse, is usually researched and discussed in categories like "informal" and "nonstandard." These terms refer to different forms of little-regulated, barely codified, and therefore highly unprotected and vulnerable work in dependent, changing positions. The range of work includes migrant, seasonal, and casual labor, usually with extremely low remuneration, in positions of extreme dependency, and mostly linked to other activities as well as other types of income that need to be put in a family context, since one cannot survive on just one of these income sources. This type of capitalistically influenced wage labor is justifiably regarded as highly precarious, and it is performed by workers of both genders (most frequently by women), also by many children, in the export-oriented agricultural and foodstuffs industries, in workshops and factories, and for a wide variety of services, often in slums, under conditions of extreme insecurity, and in the face of great and growing inequality. Entrepreneurs, businesses, and factories—including many multinational concerns with headquarters in the "global North"—contribute to the spread of these precarious working conditions through targeted "outsourcing." They supply goods for cheap mass consumption in affluent countries. In Asia, Africa, and Latin America, they make use of low-paid workers, often without formally hiring them, and often with the help of intermediary contractors, subcontractors, or agents. Legal protections, to the extent they even exist, are frequently half hearted and frequently circumvented or ignored. State authorities are often too weak, too partisan, or too corrupt to proceed effectively against such practices. The category of those working "informally" is difficult to demarcate and nearly impossible to register statistically. Rough estimates indicate a billion worldwide, with the trend on the rise.[32]

In Europe and North America, the "labor question" has long since lost the agitating character it once possessed as a force that stirred up radical protest and unsettled the class society of the nineteenth and twentieth century. In western Europe, excoriating the immiseration of the working class or the alienation of labor has long since ceased to hold the central place in the critique of capitalism it once occupied. But this interpretation is conditioned by the fragmentation along national or regional lines of the mental maps that continue to dominate our minds. If it were possible to make a truly global perspective the basis for our moral conscience, sense of social commitment, and political demands (something that would contravene not only ingrained habits but also weighty interests in the global North), the "labor question" would now suddenly reappear as the "labor question of the global South": morally challenging, an urgent problem of social justice, hard to change, but not hopeless. From a historical perspective, three questions obtrude:

1. The categorization of this labor as "informal" or "nonstandard" depends on contrasting such labor with a model of constant, regulated, codified work that is assumed to be "formal" or "standard." Yet not only does this supposed "standard" represent just a small minority phenomenon in most societies of the global South, usually in state-related employment; in any historical long-term perspective that includes the global North it is also the exception, and even in the twentieth century it was not "normal" in many places, but at best what used to be (and frequently still is) the norm. If one takes this seriously, one can hardly avoid questioning the very categories "nonstandard" and "informal." Yet they are hard to replace.

2. The situation in the global South undoubtedly poses burdensome problems that were absent from the phase of industrial capitalism's rise in Europe and North America. One problem in particular is the oppressive dependence of a large part of the work performed on site upon multinational chains and corporations, a dependence associated with postcolonial inequality between

producers in the South and consumers (including processing and downstream manufacturers) in the North. Nevertheless, wage labor of the "informal," poorly paid, unprotected, precarious kind has always existed in Europe, too. It was a mass phenomenon in eighteenth- and nineteenth-century Europe, but it persisted as a phenomenon on the margins of European society in the second half of the twentieth and the beginning of the twenty-first century. Yet it was pushed back by regulated forms of wage labor and, above all, significantly defused. For this to happen, economic growth was an irreplaceable precondition. Another contributing factor was the institutionalization of wage labor *inside enterprises* as something internal to capitalism. Pressure that emanated from labor movements also carried weight. But, above all, laws, ordinances, and governmental controls played a decisive role.

3. If this ocean of informal labor is viewed globally together with the aforementioned tendencies toward "informalization" that have also been gaining ground in the economically most developed societies, then one can understand how—parallel to the financialization of capitalism since the 1970s, and closely associated with this trend—the "informality" or "informalization" of wage labor represents a global challenge not likely to fade away anytime soon. Ultimately, this trend, like financialization, results from the increasingly pervasive application of the increasingly

dominant principles of the market to ever more areas of economy and society under conditions of digitalized worldwide communication. Alleviating the major social problems that result from this trend will not succeed without forceful intervention from strong states and their cooperation.

Market and State

In the controversies that have surrounded capitalism, state and market are usually regarded as antipodes, and for good reason. Market action and governmental-political action are indeed beholden to different logics, especially in the democratic era. Each one has a different foundation on which its legitimacy rests: unequally distributed ownership rights on one side, equal citizenship rights on the other. They follow different procedures: there one of exchange, here a process of debate with the aim of building consensus and deciding by majority. There money is the most important medium; here, by contrast, it is power. The pursuit of particular advantages is the clear goal of market action, even if it can be claimed, along with Adam Smith, that this indirectly serves general utility. Attainment of the general welfare, by contrast, is the aim of politics, even if it is clear that the content of this public good only emerges out of the political process, and even if it is conceded that it is legitimate to pursue particular interests within the framework of the democratic decision-making process. Since the eighteenth century, liberal constitutional orders have justified restricting the autonomy of both spheres. They have tied the exercise of political power first to constitutional and then to democratic foundations, and deliberately not to economic resources. At the same time, however, they have secured the right to own property, and everything that ensues from ownership, as a basic right, and have therefore removed it from the grasp of political and state power, no matter how large the constitutional leeway remains for arranging the relationship of market to state in different ways. In constitutional states, political power and the economic resources that ensue from property rights limit each other reciprocally: this is a very fundamental aspect of the separation of powers that contributes to the guarantee of liberty.

Over and over again, there have been political configurations in which the opposition between (more) state and (more) market represented the main controversy. This is how the issue was posed in the epochal conflict between the state-run, centrally administered economy and the capitalist market economy during the Cold War. It has been a similar divide at issue in the debates about "neoliberalism," deregulation, and privatization since the 1980s.

Nonetheless, it would be wrong to conceive of market and state exclusively as antipodes. Although, as the foregoing account has tried to show, a certain institutional differentiation between market and state, between economy and government policy, is among the preconditions for any form of capitalism, a close tie between market and state, between economy and state policy, has historically been the rule in one form or another: the variations on this tie have ranged from the practically symbiotic relationship between high finance and power during the Middle Ages, through the close interlinking of state formation with market formation in early modern Europe, and subsequent government intervention aimed at the social regulation of wage labor in the nineteenth and twentieth centuries, to the increased demand for state intervention as a result of capitalism's recent financialization. This series of examples could be extended to include the important role of government policy in implementing and expanding capitalism in the East Asian "tiger states" starting in the 1950s and 1960s and to the more or less dictatorial or authoritarian state institutions in China and Russia over the last several decades.

We may, especially with a view to the West, distinguish among three unequally long phases for the nineteenth and twentieth centuries,[33] and it looks as if a fourth one has just begun. In response to the tight fusion of market and state in the early modern era, which Adam Smith was up in arms against, the at-core liberal revolutions and reforms of the Atlantic world in the late eighteenth and early nineteenth centuries ushered in a phase of relative separation between market and state. States held back from taking an interventionist stance on economic and social welfare policy until the 1870s and 1880s. They promoted the self-propelling dynamism of market economies at the same time that they left these market economies to their own devices. Talk of weak "night-watchman states" is, to be sure, completely misleading. In fact, it was during those decades that nation-states, which were to some extent just emerging and to some extent developing into powerful entities, first really gained domestic and foreign agenda-setting powers. The contributions made by states to economic and social development were considerable; one need only think of the expansion in infrastructure and education, neither one of which most governments simply abandoned to the free play of market forces. Yet a policy of economic liberalism and deregulation under the banner of free trade was the appropriate fit for the kind of competition between mostly small businesses that was barely controlled and for a workforce that was still hardly organized. Although some protective regulation arrived with the "Factory Acts" and similar regulations (1833 in England, later in other countries), state support for welfare remained minimal, and the liberal belief in the freedom of the individual as something useful for all remained strong.

The 1870s and 1880s brought about a change of trend. The change was, on the one hand, a reaction to the serious international crisis of capitalism in the 1870s. On the other hand, it was also a response to growing social tensions and especially to the rise of the organized labor movement. The shift also fit in with the trend toward concentration, mergers, and comprehensive organization typical of the managerial capitalism that was emerging in the last quarter of the nineteenth century and increasingly augmenting the older kind of ownership capitalism. As was demonstrated by a renewal of interventionism in economic policy (e.g., nationalized industries), by growing public spending, but also by initiatives in foreign economic policy that accompanied the implementation of imperialism (protectionist tariffs, subsidies, zones of influence, and colonies established also for economic purposes), and especially by the rise of the welfare state starting in the 1880s, state authorities were now intervening with greater intensity in economy and society, just as, conversely, economic and social interests that had become increasingly organized were now exercising influence on politics and public policy through their lobbies and interest groups. In place of the relative distance between market and state cultivated by economic liberalism during the preceding phase of capitalism, the decades prior to the First World War now witnessed an increasingly tight interdependence between market and state under the banner of the "organization" principle. There was talk of "organized" and also of "co-ordinated" or "controlled capitalism," whose foundations had already been laid in the decades prior to 1914.[34]

Political and economic forces driving expansion were tightly linked in the epochal phenomenon of imperialism, whose tension-filled rise since the 1880s contributed mightily to the outbreak of the First and Second World Wars. The First World War promoted a comprehensive non-market organization of capitalism in every one of the belligerent states, even if this was only partial and transitory. The protectionism of the interwar period widened once again the distance separating the twentieth century from the era of classical liberal free trade. The world economic crisis of the 1930s strengthened anew the inclination of states to intervene in economic and social processes. This renewed interventionism assumed a severely undemocratic guise in the dictatorships of Europe and Japan, but it took on a democratic form in the American New Deal, which in the 1930s laid the groundwork for a welfare state even in the United States. After the Second World War, to be sure, the war economy's compulsory measures were abolished and its protectionist encrustations dismantled step by step. But in other respects—the expansion of the welfare state and labor legislation, cooperation between organized interests and state agencies, economic policy increasingly tailored to Keynesian standards, a stronger role for nationalized sectors and government planning overall, rudiments of intergovernmental coordination at the global level—the third quarter of the twentieth century was the high point of *organized capitalism*. This thorough entanglement of market and state prompted talk about a "mixed economy"—a term that drew a dual line of demarcation, distinguishing this order both from the laissez-faire capitalism of yore and from the centrally administered economic system under Soviet hegemony. During the third quarter of the twentieth century, there were many in the West as well who believed they were on the way into a postcapitalist phase. Yet realism was on the side of those observers who diagnosed a new stage of capitalist development and talked about "organized capitalism," "coordinated capitalism," or even "welfare capitalism." The Cold War gave this debate additional momentum. For the Communist challenge repeatedly stimulated an interest in capitalism's capacity for reform.[35]

In the late 1970s there began a phase of "revived market capitalism" (Charles Maier). "Neoliberal" theories prizing the self-regulating forces of the market gained force, a deliberate thrust toward deregulation and privatization took place along with a certain retrenchment in social welfare services to reverse the major trend line of the previous decades. At the same time, the revival ushered in a shift in emphasis from organized labor to the side of capital. One of the causes of this change in direction was undoubtedly the economic crisis of the 1970s, which forcefully demonstrated the limits of the system of organized capitalism that had been dominant up to then by presenting policy makers with the double problem of mass unemployment and monetary erosion ("stagflation"). Among the fundamental causes deserving special mention is the rapid growth of global competition, which placed the old industrial countries with their high wage and labor costs under considerable pressure. It also happened that the functioning of organized capitalism in the antecedent decades presupposed a degree of social consensus that was increasing eroding in some countries, notably England. Since the end of the 1970s, the United Kingdom, soon joined by the United States, became the country pioneering this change of course. But the zeitgeist had also changed, away from organization and solidarity as leading values, and toward individualization and appreciating diversity and spontaneity. The rapid rise of consumer capitalism fit in with this trend. The collapse of the Eastern bloc was interpreted as proof that market forces were superior to planning. That collapse, moreover, removed the great challenge of a noncapitalist alternative. During the Cold War, the presence of such an alternative had increased the willingness of some representatives of capital and many political actors to be more responsive toward workers' demands and to back a more welfare-conscious social market economy as a way of forestalling more radical changes.

But it did not come to a real rollback of the state; quite the contrary. On the European continent, and all the more so in East Asia, the Anglo-American neoliberal model was followed only reluctantly or not at all. The dismantling of social services in Germany, for example, was kept within very narrow limits even in the last decade of the twentieth and first decade of the twenty-first century; the frequently invoked *Wende* ("turning point") in German economic and social policy never took place. There as elsewhere, resistance to the neoliberalization of capitalism remained unbroken, public spending high. Yet *deregulation* gained ground internationally, especially in the field of finance and as part of the more general financialization of the economy that set in.[36]

Whether the international financial crisis since 2008 has ended the phase of "revived market capitalism" and started a fourth phase of modern capitalism's history remains to be seen. The crisis has profoundly shaken the foundations of neoliberalism's legitimation, both political and intellectual. For, without a doubt, deregulation of the financial sector was an important cause of the financial economy's collapse in 2008, which started in the leading countries embracing radical market finance capitalism, the United States and England. And the core convictions of neoliberalism—autonomy and the self-regulating capacity of markets—were disclaimed and discredited by the key actors of finance capitalism themselves in the crisis of 2008 as these capitalists practically pleaded with national governments to stave off their final collapse, which governments—using the argument "too big to fail"—then did. As a consequence, public debt grew by leaps and bounds. The financial market crisis of capitalism was transformed into a public debt crisis, with damaging consequences whose end is not yet in sight, especially in Europe. The self-disenchantment of the neoliberal myth about the market's self-healing powers could not have been more thoroughgoing.

Yet the consequences are by no means clear. Certain tendencies to reregulation of the financial sector have been introduced, in individual countries as well as internationally. Yet the influence of the interested parties affected thereby is great, and that influence is impeding many a conceivable solution. The subject matter is complicated. Above all, the power to make and implement political decisions are not nearly strong enough *at the supranational level*, although this would be necessary in order to tame a finance capitalism that has long been globally active.

Whoever wants to compare different types of contemporary capitalism will usually select the different relationships of market to state as the central criterion distinguishing different "varieties of capitalism" from each other.[37] And indeed, the relationship of market to state varies greatly from country to country. Without making any claim to being exhaustive, this may be illustrated with a few examples.

A kind of organized capitalism with strong state intervention also developed in the United States during the twentieth century. But it showed up in America more under the guise of regulation to secure competition (prohibitions on cartels, antitrust policy), and also in the form of a military-industrial complex linking private enterprise with the state. While the American version also included government-facilitated financing of mass consumption through easy credit, it had less to do with the provision of welfare services by the state or with government intervention into the internal affairs of companies. Sweden, by contrast, proved that a very competitive capitalism is compatible not only with a functioning democracy, but also with state-regulated cooperation between classes, values oriented toward collective solidarity, and a high level of welfare state services. Even if in Sweden, too, the "neoliberal" about-face starting in the 1980s was tantamount to a certain streamlining of the welfare state, there was not nearly such a far-reaching cutback of social services there as there was in England at the same time. In Germany, which may be regarded as the motherland of organized capitalism in the late nineteenth and twentieth centuries, a variety of "Rhenish capitalism" started to develop in the 1950s that also included a great deal of state-supported coordination and a pronounced welfare state orientation (the "social market economy"). Yet postwar German economic policy had many fewer instances of direct interventionism than did Sweden or France at the same time, and there was much greater respect for the self-regulating capacity of civil society than, for example, in Japan. There industrialization only started in the late nineteenth century, under very strong state guidance from the outset, although the state's planning and management authorities cooperated closely with the country's gigantic private enterprises, the *zaibatsu*, and gave a powerful push to the development of technology, industry, and exports. At the same time, authorities in this country of weak trade unions and enterprises that took care of everything largely dispensed with the development of a comprehensive welfare state.

Through resolute policies promoting exports, critical investments in training, and high macroeconomic savings rates, Hong Kong and Taiwan started to industrialize in the 1950s, Singapore and South Korea in the 1960s. They clearly embarked on a course of capitalism and the market economy, but without exception involving intensive support and guidance by the state. Singapore's authoritarian governmental structure, like that of South Korea's at the outset, was much more conducive than cumbersome to industrialization. China's modernization in the post-Maoist era rested, on the one hand, on the market-oriented energies of broad sections of the population no longer subjected to constrictions. On the other hand, something like a "revolution from above" also occurred. The capitalist dynamism that quickly gathered pace was initiated and guided by party cadres and state functionaries, but they were aiming at a limited release of entrepreneurial activity and, to this extent, at a certain self-restriction by the state. The items on the Chinese modernization agenda included privatizing some state enterprises, melting away the Maoist welfare state and the security it guaranteed, and unleashing a massive rural-to-urban migration that produced exploitation and privation on a scale recalling Europe's early industrialization. Workers protested against social decline, exploitation, and insecurity by holding up pictures of Mao in admonition, while their Communist government was taking advice from the upper echelons of North American finance capitalism and enlisting the resources, networks, and patriotism of Chinese living abroad. China has developed a state-monitored industrial capitalism resting on low wages, hard exploitation of workers, and mass exports that quickly led to great economic success, immense riches in the hands of a few, and also to a great deal of protest. The influence of the state on this kind of industrialization remained strong, although it is abating a little. Most banks, energy and communication enterprises as well as firms in other strategic branches remain state-owned or at least state-controlled, there is no free market for real estate, and government interventions permeate both the economy and civil society. Wages are low by international standards, yet since 2005 they have also been growing in relative terms. On the whole, most Chinese are doing better today than thirty years ago. The repressiveness of the political system is pronounced, but it is exercised selectively and guardedly with regard to the actors involved in economic growth. Overall, this is an experiment demonstrating once again the variety of political conditions under which capitalism—at least for a time—can flourish. But only time will tell how compatible market and state are under authoritarian-dictatorial conditions in the long run. In Russia, the transition to capitalism in the 1990s led to the state partially withdrawing itself from the economy, but also to economic retrogression, unprecedented inequality, and major social damage until around 2003, when a strong trend toward reinvigorating the influence of the state became evident. By way of comparison, India has on the whole been following a rather liberal course economically for a good two decades.[38]

State interventions have been indispensable for the emergence, expansion, and survival of capitalism, as this historical overview shows. Government interventions into capitalist market economies are likely to become even more important over the coming years and decades. There are three systemic reasons why the need for state intervention has always been strong and will probably continue to grow.

1. Markets, which make capitalistic conduct possible in the first place, presuppose framework conditions that can only be established by political means. Markets cannot do the job of removing barriers to commerce (e.g., feudal obstacles such as guild regulations, trade monopolies and privileges, fines and tolls on travel) that fragment and constrain, of guaranteeing a minimum of peaceful order, and of providing rules to conclude and implement contracts or contract-like agreements. Without the use of political power, capitalism would never have taken off, nor can it take off in the future. Often the preconditions for the existence of supraregional markets resulted from the use of force—in war, for example, or in the course of colonization.

2. A growing instability of capitalist processes can be discerned, to the extent that these processes have become detached over the last several decades from the restrictive but also stabilizing grounds in which they were once embedded and have, moreover, become internally differentiated.

This was illustrated above in the case of two different transitions, first from ownership to managerial capitalism, and then with the shift to capitalism's current phase of financialization. In the second transition, the investment function has been so powerfully detached from its ties to other functions (such as management of the enterprise or personnel policy) that it has become an independent force, carried away to the point of self-destruction unless the investment function can be recaptured and reembedded. In the search for new ways of embedding finance, state guidelines and controls need not play the only role. Civil society-based arrangements become increasingly relevant, but strong and effective government intervention remains indispensable. (The problem is posed in a somewhat different way, however, outside the North Atlantic area, where widespread clientelism, patronage, and corruption—in other words, special ways of "embedding" economic institutions in community, society, and politics—lead to features of the system that have been characterized and criticized with such catchwords as "patrimonial capitalism" and "crony capitalism.")[39]

3. Capitalism, even in its advanced stages, develops in a way that has disruptive and destructive effects on its social, cultural, and political environment and can call into question its social acceptance. Here one need only recall the

profound crises, repeated with a certain inevitability, that have a habit of starting out as financial crises, as in 1873, 1929–1930 und 2007–2008, yet leave in their wake serious repercussions for the "real economy," impair the welfare of broad sectors of the population, and possibly lead to social and political disruptions. In equal measure, though, attention must be drawn to the long-term polarizing effects of capitalism when it has been successful. By this I do not mean only the well-known connection between industrialization, wage labor, and worker protest, which leads to social polarization when not counteracted by welfare state measures. Rather, it is also important to mention what is demonstrated by certain findings from the early modern Netherlands, from the process of industrialization in the nineteenth century, and from experiences over the last several decades. These different findings all show that capitalist growth, if not counteracted with compensatory measures, does not necessarily lead to massive impoverishment—quite the contrary!—but does go hand in hand with increasing income and wealth inequality. Exorbitantly high managerial earnings, whose lead over average incomes in the last several decades has reached dizzying heights, are just a tiny, though quite visible and especially irritating, aspect of an increase in inequality that is quite complex. Especially in democratic political cultures, this surge in inequality is perceived as unjust, and over the long run it can call into question the legitimacy of the system.[40]

Historical experiences show that the destabilizing social consequences of capitalism can at least be alleviated by governmental measures if a body politic is strong enough and capable of mobilizing such measures, even in the face of resistance, and implementing them with a sense of proportion. In this regard, there is a growing need over the long run for compensatory and preventive intervention by the state, especially since the politically active public in many countries has become more sensitive, more articulate, and with a higher level of aspirations, and this critical public is likely to express its concerns even more in the future. Political systems, however, often have only a limited capacity for producing the services that are actually necessary. It is obvious that such factors as the existence or lack of a protest culture, the political public's level of development, and the peculiarities of each political system are very decisive in determining whether economic and social grievances lead to social movements and government interventions that, should they prove successful, enhance capitalism's social acceptability and hence also its capacity for survival. The rise of the welfare state since the late nineteenth century is the best example of how this works. Today an analogous process for civilizing capitalism is impeded by the lack of a match between an increasingly global capitalism operating across borders and the organization of political power still largely structured around national states. We are a long way from any kind of transnational global sovereignty that could really check capitalism's persistently vigorous dynamism with countervailing force: this mismatch continues to pose an unsolved problem.

5

Analysis and Critique

The concept of capitalism began as a term expressing difference. It only made sense to the extent that it distinguished what it was describing from observable or imaginable alternatives. Over and over again, the concept has been filled with life by contrasting it with something else, usually with some kind of socialism. Today, it is frequently unclear which tangible or imaginable alternatives capitalism could or should be distinguished from. Perhaps this results in some difficulties attending the concept, especially its sometimes almost all-embracing character.

The concept emerged as an instrument of critique and analysis at one and the same time. Over and over again, it drew its power and attractiveness from this dual function, which continues to characterize the concept until today. But often the dual function resulted in ambiguity and partisanship that burdened the concept as an instrument of scholarly analysis.

On the one hand, more and more authors find the concept useful, including many historians, at least in some languages such as English and German and in some countries like the United States.[1] Especially when it comes to discussing complex connections among economic, social, political, and cultural dimensions of historical reality, and to synthesizing or making broad comparisons across space and time, the concept has distinct advantages.

On the other hand, the concept continues to serve as an interpretive concept that invites fundamental debate about past, present, and future. It certainly plays a role in intellectual and political debates outside the scholarly world, too. As in its early period around 1900, the concept also opens up a view to the big questions of the time and to fundamental problems of contemporary civilization.

By no means does the concept always have a negative connotation. On the contrary, it can also be used with an emphatically positive valuation. As far as Milton Friedman was concerned, for example, there was no doubt about that. In 1962 he conceived of "competitive capitalism— the organization of the bulk of economic activity through private enterprise operating in a free market—as a system of economic freedom and a necessary condition for political freedom." In 1997 Gary Becker concurred without any qualification: "Capitalism with free markets is the most effective system yet devised for raising both economic well-being and political freedom. 'Chicago' economics argued this for many decades, but it took the dramatic end of communism to show that what is true in theory and in the past also holds in the modern world." Both economists were influential exponents of the "neoliberal" Chicago school and were awarded for their scholarly work with the Nobel Prize in Economic Sciences. In popular literature, too, the term *capitalism* is used in a positive sense.[2]

Anyone who takes a serious look at the history of capitalism and, moreover, knows something about life in centuries past that were either not capitalist or barely so, cannot but be impressed by the immense progress that has taken place in large parts of the world (although not in all!). There has been progress above all for the many people who are not members of a well-situated upper class, progress with respect to material living conditions and overcoming poverty, gains in life span and health, opportunities for choice, and freedom.[3] It was progress of which one may say, in retrospect, that it would presumably not have happened without capitalism's characteristic way of constantly stirring things up, pressing them forward, and reshaping them. And whoever would rather invoke different explanatory factors, like the growth of knowledge, technological change, or industrialization, as the real motors of progress should recall that, so far, any industrialization successful over the long run has everywhere presupposed capitalism. Capitalism's principles, moreover, have also done much to disseminate knowledge, which can be seen from the history of the media, starting early with the printing of books, through the political press, to today's Internet. Thus far, all alternatives to capitalism have proven inferior, both with respect to the creation of prosperity and the facilitation of freedom. The downfall of centrally administered Communist economies in the last third of the twentieth century was, in this respect, a key process for evaluating the historical balance sheet of capitalism.

Nevertheless, whoever talks or writes seriously about capitalism seldom ignores its dark sides, which are at least mentioned if not put at the forefront. The critique of capitalism, at least in the West, enjoys a long tradition. But it is also current. Interestingly, it is readily formulated in discussions about the possible or anticipated end of capitalism.[4]

Some themes in the critique of capitalism that were once at the center of attention have, however, moved to the margins. Catholic social teaching continues to warn against the " 'idolatry' of the market" and "radical capitalistic ideology" (according to *Centesimus Annus*, the papal encyclical of 1991). Yet this is miles away from the fundamental critique of capitalism that had been promoted for centuries by the Roman Catholic Church. Although the current pope, undoubtedly against the background of his experiences with countries from the global South, has again intensified the tone of the Catholic critique.

The right-wing radical and racist critique of capitalism familiar since the 1870s, and reaching a high point under German National Socialism with its illiberal connotations and anti-Semitic thrust, is not currently much in vogue, at least not in Western societies. Still, it is alive and can easily be revitalized.

The immiseration of the working class is not laid at the doorstep of capitalism any longer, even by the political left in countries like Germany. The "labor question" has ceased to divide society in the more affluent parts of the world, even if it can (and should) be rediscovered at the global level. Things have also become downright quiet around the critique of alienated labor in capitalism. That critique has lost its edge now that individualized production by work groups, with some scope for workers to design the workplace, is promoted by capitalist enterprises in the post-Fordist era, and creativity is not only upheld as an attribute of skill but also demanded on the market. It seems as if capitalism, by using accommodation to evade much of the criticism once directed against it, is capable of just enough change, so that a good bit of the critique comes to naught.[5]

It is impossible to overlook the way that economic interests, and especially the sales and profits interests of the armaments industry, play an important role in charging international tensions and preparing for wars. Yet scholarship today is a long way from explaining the outbreak of wars primarily by economic factors and attributing armed conflicts mainly to the contradictions of capitalism. Instead, scholarship repeatedly refers to the interest capitalists have in peace—as a precondition for doing business successfully.[6] Imperialism theories in the tradition of Luxemburg or Lenin are not currently in great demand. Here is another example: it has become rare to chalk up the rise and triumph of German and Italian fascism to the supporters of a monopolistic bourgeoisie helping Mussolini and Hitler into the saddle of power, or to the internal contradictions of capitalism. Certainly, the support of major portions of the conservative elites (including many industrialists) for Hitler in the final crisis of the Weimar Republic does stick in one's memory, along with the profitable cooperation of "big business" with the Nazi war economy. Yet it has since become not only well known, but also better recollected, how resolute and diverse were the very large sections of German society who "worked towards the Führer" (in Ian Kershaw's memorable phrase). That wide spectrum of society identifying with the regime

makes it is easy to see through the exculpatory simplifica-
tion ascribing liability for the triumph of National Socialism and its catastrophic consequences entirely to the account of the capitalists. This leaves undisturbed the insight
that the victory of German National Socialism would have
been unlikely without the great crisis of capitalism at the
beginning of the 1930s.[7]

The contemporary critique of capitalism is multifac-
eted. Concrete abuses are denounced, such as "structured
irresponsibility" in the financial sector.[8] That lack of accountability has led to a widening gap—incidentally, in
violation of one of capitalism's central premises—between
deciding, on the one hand, and answering for the consequences of decisions, on the other. As a result, exorbitant profits for money managers are facilitated by public
budgets that take on gigantic losses ("too big to fail"). The
contemporary critique of growing inequality as a consequence of capitalism is, moreover, becoming ever more
urgent. Here, public discussion has focused on the kind of
income and wealth inequality that since the 1970s has
become much more severe inside most individual countries; there has been less interest in the much more serious inequality that exists between countries and regions
of the globe. The latter grew exorbitantly between 1800
and 1950, but no more since then.[9] Lamenting growing
inequality blends into protest against infringements on
distributive justice, which is how the critique becomes
systemically relevant. Also lamented are the perennial insecurity, unrelenting acceleration pressures, and extreme
individualization that are inherent in capitalism and that

may lead, absent countermeasures, to the erosion of social welfare and neglect of the public interest. This raises the question of just what it is that holds societies together.

Similar in the way it poses fundamental questions is the critique of capitalism's constitutive dependence on permanent growth and constant expansion beyond the attained status quo, a dependence that threatens to destroy natural resources (environment, climate) and cultural resources (solidarity, meaning), resources that, by the way, capitalism also presupposes in order to survive.[10] This, in turn, raises the anxious question of where the limits of the market and venality lie or where—on moral or practical grounds—they should be drawn.[11] Strong arguments for the case that there is a need for such boundaries—that capitalism, in other words, cannot be allowed to permeate everything, but that it needs noncapitalist abutments in society, culture, and the state—may be elicited from the history of capitalism. At the most fundamental level, the discrepancy between the claim of democratic politics to shape and communicate universalized values, on the one hand, and the dynamic of capitalism that evades democratic politics, on the other, remains an enduring problem. Finally, one cannot overlook a form of totalizing critique that rejects "capitalism" as the symbolic epitome of (Western) modernity or as the outright embodiment of evil.[12]

The historical overview presented here shows the immense mutability of capitalism across the centuries. The critique of capitalism, in tandem with social and political movements, has been an important motor driving its changes, as was shown above, especially in the section on work in capitalism and the one on market and state. Criticism can also be a motor of change in the future. For capitalism does not get to decide about the sociopolitical conditions under which it develops. It can flourish in different political systems, even under dictatorial rule—at least for a time; the affinity between capitalism and democracy is less pronounced than was long hoped and assumed. Capitalism does not set its own goals from its own resources. It can be useful for different social and political goals. Among these goals, presumably, is the aim of rerouting the economy in the direction of greater renewability and sustainability. But this can only happen *if* enough political pressure, and political decisions to match, are mobilized in favor of such goals. That does not seem to be on the horizon, either in the prosperous societies of the global North or worldwide, at this time. Capitalism lives off its social, cultural, and political embedding, as much as it simultaneously threatens and corrodes these moorings. It can be influenced by political means and those of civil society *when and if* these are strong and decisive enough.

Seen from this perspective, one could say that, every era, every region, and every civilization gets the capitalism it deserves. Currently, considered alternatives *to* capitalism are hard to identify. But *within* capitalism, very different variants and alternatives can be observed, and even more of them can be imagined. It is *their* development that matters. The reform of capitalism is a permanent task. In this, the critique of capitalism plays a central role.

Notes

Chapter 1: What Does Capitalism Mean?

1. "In History Departments, It's Up with Capitalism," *New York Times*, 6 Apr. 2013; Sklansky 2012; Kocka 2010. Many people have supported me with suggestions and information in preparing this book. They are gratefully acknowledged in the German edition (in the first endnote of the opening chapter). In preparing the English-language edition, I benefited especially from the advice and assistance of Knut Borchardt, Richard R. John, Michael Merrill, Jerry Z. Muller, the late Gerhard A. Ritter, and James J. Sheehan. I had the chance to present my views in seminars organized by Victoria de Grazia at Columbia, by Harold James at Princeton, and by a group of graduate students at Stanford. Special thanks are owed Jeremiah Riemer for his sympathetic translation, which resulted in fruitful collaboration and substantive clarifications, and to the research center Work and Human Lifecycle in Global History at the Humboldt University of Berlin for wide-ranging assistance.

2. Hilger 1982, 408–42, esp. 410, 433f., 437 (quotes from German sources 1776, 1756, 1717, 1808 and 1813). On the following, see also Kocka 2015.

3. Blanc 1850, 161; Proudhon 1851, 223. *Grand dictionnaire universel du XIXe siècle* (Paris: Larousse, 1867), 3:320. Liebknecht cited by Hilger 1982, 444. (An English translation of Liebknecht's remarks by Erich Hahn may be found in William A. Pelz, ed., Wilhelm Liebknecht and German Social Democracy: A Documentary History [Westport, CT: 1994], 2; http://plato.acadiau.ca/courses/germ/voss/2813-23/BattlefieldsofIndustry.htm.)

4. Hilger 1982, 443 on Rodbertus; Schäffle 1870, 116. *Meyers Konversations-Lexikon*, 3rd ed. (Leipzig: Bibliographisches Institut, 1876), 9:876; Sombart 1902; overview in Passow 1927.

5. Jones 1851, 646 (I owe this reference to Michael Merrill). Hobson 1894; Shadwell 1920, 69; *Encyclopaedia Britannica* 1910–1911 (11th ed.), 5:278; and 1922 (12th ed.), 30 (Suppl.):565–71. Williams 1976, 42–44.

6. Veblen, 1914, 282–83; Brick 2006, 23–33; Merrill 1990, 470–73; Merrill 2014.

7. E.g., Salvioli 1906; Pirenne 1914; Cunningham, 1916; Tawney 1926; Sée 1926.

8. The standard edition is *MEW* XXIII–XXV Karl Marx, (= *Das Kapital* I–III (1867, 1884–1885, and 1894); Marx had already worked out a brief summary in his "Lohnarbeit und Kapital" (1849), *MEW* VI, 397–423; "Manifest der Kommunistischen Partei" (1848), *MEW* IV, 459–93. A very good introduction is provided by Muller 2003, 166–207. The English titles from *MECW (Marx/Engels Collected Works)* are the three volumes of Capital, "Wage Labor and Capital," and the "Manifesto of the Communist Party"—all of which may be found online at https://www.marxists.org/archive/marx/works/cw.

9. Weber's statements on capitalism come from different periods of his life and are spread throughout his oeuvre. Most important are his book-length essay *The Protestant Ethic and the Spirit of Capitalism*, his encyclopedic multivolume opus *Economy and Society*, and his *General Economic History*. See Weber 1978 (2013), esp. 63–166, 351–54, 1094–110; Weber 1927 (repr. 1950), esp. 275–369; Weber 2010. A good introduction to his views on capitalism: Schluchter 2009, 63–87 (quote 81); English-language passage of Schluchter citing Weber from an earlier, overlapping study by Schluchter 1989, 346 and note 108; and see again Weber 1978, 111, on the "fundamental and . . . unavoidable element of irrationality" of economic systems); further: Swedberg 1998; Ghosh 2008.

10. Schumpeter 1961, 70; Schumpeter 1939, 223 (definition); Schumpeter 1947, 81–86 ("creative destruction"). See McCraw 2007.

11. Esp. in Schumpeter 1947, pt. 2.

12. Keynes 1927, 50; Keynes 1936, 161 ff., 163; Akerlof/Shiller 2009; Berghoff 2011, esp. 80–86.

13. Polanyi 1944. Closely following him: Streeck 2009. For historians' critique of Polanyi: Kindleberger 1974; Eisenberg 2011, 62–66.

14. Braudel 1982/84, II (*The Wheels of Commerce*) and III (*The Perspective of the World*), 619–32. See Vries 2012. On monopoly capitalism: Baran/Sweezy 1966; Cowling/Tomlinson 2012.

15. Hilferding 1910; Luxemburg 1968; Lenin 1920.

16. Wallerstein 1974, 1980, 1989, and 2011; Arrighi 1994 and 2007.

17. See e.g. Christian 2004, 446–81; Osterhammel 2014, 667–672; Sanyal 2007; Frieden 2007; Beckert 2014.

18. In this context see Parthasarathi 2008; Maier 2011.

19. See Mann I, 1993, 23 ff.: Capitalism includes commodity production, private property owning the means of production, and free wage labor separated from ownership of the means of production. Fulcher 2004: Capitalism is based on investments intended to make a profit. Boltanski/Chiapello 1999, 37 ff.: the chief feature of capitalism that lends the system its dynamic for change consists in the way that capital aiming at profit maximization—that is, at increasing each amount of newly invested capital—is plowed back into economic circulation over and over again. Appleby 2010, 20–26: capitalism as a "cultural system" based on economic conduct in which the drive of private investors to obtain profits is central. Ingham 2011, 53: for him, the essential elements of capitalism are a monetary system that permits the creation of money through bank credit for investment purposes; market and exchange; and private enterprises producing commodities. Swanson 2012, 5: capitalism is "an economic system in which the owners of the means of production hire wage laborers to produce goods and services in order to sell in the market for a profit."—L. Neal, "Introduction", in Neal/Williamson 2014, I:1–23, esp. 2: four elements are common in different concepts of capitalism: private property rights; contracts enforceable by third parties; markets with responsive prices; and supportive governments.

20. More details in Kocka 2010 and 2015.

21. There is currently a lively debate about the question of the extent to which free wage labor should be included as a defining feature of "capitalism." See van der Linden 2008 and below, p. 124.

Chapter 2: Merchant Capitalism

1. Hartwell 1983, 14; Grassby 1999, 19; Fulcher 2004, 19 ff.; Pryor 2010, 8 ff.

2. On Babylonia during the second and first millennium BCE, see Jursa 2014; Graeber 2011, 235–64.

3. Finley 1973, 144 (quote); on wage labor in the ancient world: Lis/Soly 2012, pt. I; Temin 2012; Jongman 2014.

4. Mielants 2007, 47–57; Ptak 1992; Lu 1992; Li 2004.

5. Chaudhuri 2005, 34–51, 203–20; Spuler 1952, 400–11; Rodinson 2007, 63–65, 82–85; Bernstein 2008, 66–76.

6. Udovitsch 1970; Heck 2006, 41–157; Chaudhuri 2005, 211–15; Shatzmiller 2011.

7. Udovitsch 1988; Rodinson 2007, 57–90, see 60 ff. on Ibn Khaldun and 88 ff. on the question of the bourgeoisie; Graeber 2011, 271–82.

8. On the following, see Kulischer 1965, I:229–78; Howell 2010; Persson 2014.

9. Ogilvie 2011; on the following, see also North 2011, 65–102; Stark 1993.

10. On Romano Mairano, see Heynen 1905, 86–120 ; on the Medici, see de Roover 1963; on the Fuggers, see Ehrenberg 1896. In general Ashtor 1972; Carruthers/Espeland 1991.

11. Van der Wee/Kurgan-van Hentenryk 2000, 71–112.

12. See Kulischer 1965, I:215–21; Blickle 1988, 7–12, 51–58; Arrighi 2010, 103–5; van Bavel 2010, 54–57.

13. Le Goff 1956, 1986, and 2010; Muller 2003, 3–12; Kulischer 1965, I:262–74, esp. the examples on 271–74.

14. On India until 1600, see Parthasarathi 2008; Roy 2014; Subrahmanyam 1994. On Southeast Asia: Hall, 1984; on East African merchant economies, Middleton 2009; Mielants 2007, 86–124; Bernstein 2008, 103 ff.

15. See Abu-Lughod 1989: her depiction overemphasizes the connections between the different parts of the world. See also Dunn 2012.

16. This essentially older argument (Weber, Hintze, Pomeranz, Peer Vries et al.) is found in Mielants 2007. In another version: Bin Wong/Rosenthal 2011.

17. Thus, e.g., Wood 2002.

Chapter 3: Expansion

1. *MEW* XXIII (*Das Kapital* 1), 788: "If money . . . 'comes into the world with a congenital blood-stain on one cheek,' capital comes dripping from head to foot, from every pore, with blood and dirt." (See https://www.marxists.org/archive/marx/works/1867-c1/ch31.htm for *MECW* English version of *Capital*, vol. I, ch. 31.)

2. Reinhard 2008, 28–58; Beckert 2014, chs. 2 and 3 ("War Capitalism"); on the conquistadors and their debts: Graeber 2011, 334, 465.

3. There is a controversy among economic historians as to how strongly colonial exploitation promoted European industrialization. O'Brien 1982, e.g., sees minimal influence. That the establishment of capitalism even inside Europe got a major push from colonial expansion, however, strikes me as incontrovertible. On the breakthrough of consumer capitalism in the course of early modern colonization, Trentmann 2012, pt. 2.

4. Chaudhuri 2005, 80–97; Frentrop 2002, 49–114; Reinhard 2008, 42.

5. Ehrenberg 1896, 122–24.

6. Van der Wee/Kurgan-van Hentenryk, 200, 117–264, also on the following paragraphs (quote p. 260).

7. Newton quote according to Brantlinger 1996, 44, citing the version used by Bourne 1871, 292; Kindleberger/Aliber 2005, 42, 58. On the history of company bankruptcies, Safley 2013.

8. Graeber 2011, 345.

9. Reinhard 1985, ch. 8; Reinhard 2008, 112 (quote); Appleby 2010, 121–37. The topic has been intensively researched and discussed, especially with respect to American history. See Johnson 2013; Baptist 2014; Beckert 2014, ch. 5; Zeuske 2013, 27–96. The general compatibility of capitalism and slavery is strongly emphasized. An older perspective, by contrast, places stronger emphasis on the tensions between the two (e.g., Haskell 1992). But it depends on specifying the conditions under which slavery and capitalism go together as well as the conditions under which this is not the case.

10. By way of introduction, Rösener 1993; analytically, Brenner 2007, 63–84.

11. Duplessis 1997, 76–82, 147–153.

12. De Vries/van der Woude 1997, 195–269, esp. 200 ff.; van Zanden 2009, 205–66.

13. Eisenberg 2014, 45; Duplessis 1997, 63–70, 175–84; Appleby 2010, 75–86.

14. Bücher 1927, esp. 981 f.; Thompson 1971; Schulz 2010.

15. Sokoll 1994.

16. Mendels 1972; Kriedte et al. 1981; Ogilvie/Zerman 1996.

17. Troeltsch 1897; Kisch 1989; Kulischer 1965, 2:113–137, esp. 114, 116, 123; Kriedte 1983; Medick 1996; Duplessis 1997, 88–140, esp. 215, 219; Allen 2009, 16–22; De Vries 2008.

18. Brenner 2001, esp. 224–34.

19. Numbers in Allen 2009, 17.

20. Eisenberg 2014, 73–100.

21. Schilling 2012, 634 ff. On the Weber thesis, see above, p. 12; critique of Weber thesis: Eisenberg 2009, 83–85; Schama 1987, 326–30.

22. On the older, skeptical perspectives, including literature, Muller 2003, 3–19; on the change in the eighteenth century, Appleby 2010, 87–120; a germinal work is Hirschman 1992, 105–41, esp. 106 ff.

23. Muller 2003, 51–83: introduction to Smith; a germinal work is Rothschild 2001, 116–56; different view in Vogl 2010–2011, 31–52; from a Marxist perspective, Brenner 2007.

24. Using the Netherlands as a case, Van Bavel 2010, 72–77.

25. Allen 2009, 25–79 (esp. 34, 39, 40) on "the high-wage economy of pre-industrial Britain"; Broadberry/Gupta 2006, 2–11; Clark 2005, 1308, 1311, 1319.

26. See Pomeranz 2000. Review of the debate after ten years: O'Brien 2010.; P. Vries 2013; on the weakness of proto-industrialization in Chinese (and Indian) merchant capitalism, Lu 1992, esp. 492, 496; Chaudhuri 2005, 201.

Chapter 4: The Capitalist Era

1. On the complex connection between industrialization in the West and blocked industrialization in China, India, and Africa, see Osterhammel 2014, 662 ff.; Cooper 2009 (esp. 47: African resistance to capitalism); Inikori 2002; on intra-European disparities in the nineteenth century, Berend 2013a, 462 ff.

2. Hobsbawm 1999 (reprint of 1968 ed.), p. xi; Cipolla 1973. Most comprehensive overviews of industrialization use the term

"capitalism" only marginally, if at all. See Stearns 1993; Buchheim 1994; Teich/Porter 1996; Landes 1998.

3. See Kornai 1992.

4. Marx/Engels, "Manifest der Kommunistischen Partei," *MEW* IV, 465. See https://www.marxists.org/archive/marx/works/1848/communist -manifesto/ch01.htm for English version of *Communist Manifesto*. On crises: Spree 2011; Plumpe 2010.

5. Osterhammel/Petersson 2007; Findlay/O'Rourke 2007; Mann IV:2013, 1–12.

6. Redlich 1964, 97 ff.

7. This is analyzed, using the example of the competition be-tween the family enterprise Siemens and the managerial enter-prise AEG, in Kocka 1972; on the relationship of family to business: Chandler 1977, 28 ff.; Kocka 1979; James 2006; Budde in Budde, ed. 2011, 97–115; Sabean 2011. On Rothschild: Ferguson 1999.

8. In 1950 half of the largest British enterprises were regarded as controlled by individual families (by 1970 only a third). On this, and on the meaning of family influence in large Japanese compa-nies (the *zaibatsu* and *keiretsu*), Blackford 2008, 205–16.

9. Good overview: Blackford 2008 (200 on the figures for the United States); Chandler 1977 and 1990; Folsom/McDonald 2010; Kocka 1978, 555–89; Winkler 1974.

10. Two classics: Berle/Means 1932; Burnham 1941; also see Kocka 1983.

11. This boom was, however, repeatedly interrupted—even in the decade and a half before the big collapse of 2008—by regionally contained financial crises (e.g., in the United States at the beginning of the 1990s, in Mexico 1994–1995, in East Asia and Russia 1987–1998, in Argentina 2001, and continuously in Japan).

12. James 2013, esp. 34, 37, 39 (figures); Berend, 2013b, 6 (quote), 60–80; Soros 1998, xii, xxi; Maier 2007 (locusts). Overall, Atack/Neal 2009.

13. Brilliantly exaggerated in the novel *The Fear Index* by Robert Harris (2011), esp. 81–113; Vogl 2010–2011, 83–144; autobiographi-cal, Anderson 2008.

14. http://www.imf.org/external/pubs/ft/wp/2010/data/wp10245 .zip.

15. Deutsche Bundesbank 1976, 4, 313; Sinn 2009, 32–35, 155–57.

16. Dahrendorf 2010; Bell 1979; Berend, 2013b, 91–112; Graeber 2011, ch. 12; Streeck 2014a.

17. Around 2005, funds controlled about 60 percent of the stocks in the thousand largest corporations in the United States, with 40 percent of stocks held by the twenty largest investment funds.

18. Windolf 2005 is very good on this (above all with regard to American cases); for Germany, Streeck 2009, 77–89, 230–72.

19. Wolfe 1987, ch. 10.

20. On financial market capitalism and the crisis of 2008, Berend, 2013b, esp. 60–80; Mihm/Roubini 2010.

21. Thus Van der Linden 2008, 17–61; Van der Linden 2014; for a critique, Kocka 2012.

22. See Tilly/Tilly 1998; Steinfeld 1991; Steinfeld 2001; Kocka/ Offe 2000.

23. See Stanziani 2013; Lis /Soly 2012; Ehmer 2001; Thomas 1999.

24. Tilly 1984, 33 (1550: 24 per cent; 1750: 58 per cent; 1843: 71 per cent).

25. Osterhammel 2014, 673–709; Van der Linden 2008, 20–32.

26. More details, also on the following and using German cases, Kocka 1990, 373–506.

27. See Osterhammel 2014, ch. 5: "Living Standards: Risk and Security in Material Life"; Lucassen 2006. On countervailing trends, including in the West, since the 1980s, see below, p. 140.

28. Further details in Kocka, 1990, 469–71.

29. The now classic account of early industrial England is Thompson 1963; also Thompson 1971.

30. Overview of labor movements in different countries 1870–1914: Van der Linden/Rojahn 1990. On China, Lee 2007.

31. Schmid/Protsch 2009; already a classic: Sennett 1998; in addition, Castel 2009.

32. Arnold/Bongiovi 2013; Breman 2012; already discussed in Hart 1973; Vosco et al. 2009, 1–25; Standing 2008; Kalleberg 2009. On Africa, Cooper 2009, 53 ff.; on India, Maiti/Sen 2010; on Latin America, Fernandez-Kelly/Sheffner 2006.

33. A good overview using England as an example, Fulcher 2004, 38–57.

34. See the chapters on developments in different European countries and the United States from the late nineteenth century

through the 1920s in Winkler 1974. In using the term *organized capitalism* for their discussions in this volume, the contributing authors follow Social Democratic theoretician Rudolf Hilferding, who used the concept in the 1920s. See also Crouch1993; Höpner 2004.

35. On the history of economic orders in Europe in the nineteenth and twentieth century, Berend/Shubert 2007; in the United States, Swanson 2013; in East Asia, Inkster 2001, esp. 1–20 ff. The American debates about capitalism, the "mixed economy," and the "post-capitalist order" are analyzed in Brick 2006; Lichtenstein 2006; as well as Marks 2012. See also Keynes 1927 and Shonfield 1965.

36. See Mirowski/Plehwe 2009; Harvey 2007; Krippner 2011; Berend 2013a. See also Offe 1985; Lash/Urry 1987; Crouch 2011.

37. See Hall/Soskice 2001; Amable 2003; Dore 2000; Berger/Dore 1996; Albert 1993.

38. Sketches of individual countries in Fulcher 2004, 89–134; Appleby 2010, ch. 11; Kwon 2010; Naughton 2007; Hung 2013; Myant/Drahokoupil 2010; Chandrasekhar 2010; Rendall 1997; on African Capitalism Cooper 2003 and 2009.

39. See Becker 2013, 8–9.

40. Income and wealth inequality within individual societies, to summarize roughly, increased in Europe in the nineteenth century, then decreased from the start of the twentieth century until the beginning of the 1970s, and then increased again since then. Van Zanden 1995; Van Zanden et al. 2014a.; Atkinson et al. 2010; Piketty 2014. But the link between capitalism and inequality can be influenced through measures undertaken by politics and civil society. Otherwise there would be no way of explaining why, for example, the kind of exacerbating income inequality all OECD countries have experienced has been more pronounced in some countries and very much less pronounced in others: very strongly pronounced, e.g., in the United States, Turkey, and Chile, very much weaker in Scandinavia.

Chapter 5: Analysis and Critique

1. A good overview in Sklansky 2014; see also Merrill 1995; Zakim/Kornblith 2012. Apparently there is less demand for the term *capitalism* in Spanish: R. Salvucci 2014; see esp. p. 426.

2. Friedman 1962, 4; Becker and Becker 1997, 241. Mackey 2013 speaks of "conscious capitalism liberating the heroic spirit of business." A German example: Bergheim 2007.

3. Usefully summarized in van Zanden et al. 2014b. See Vries 2013.

4. E.g., Wallerstein et al. 2013 (esp. the chapters contributed by Wallerstein); Streeck 2014b; Rifkin 2014. On historians' mostly critical views of capitalism in the second third of the twentieth century, see Ashton 1963 and Hacker 1963.

5. On this mechanism, Boltanski/Chiapello 1999.

6. E.g., Kirshner, 2007.

7. Most recently, Herbert 2014, ch. 6.; Kershaw 2008, 42–44.

8. Honegger et al. 2010.

9. On this, Milanovic 2011; Galbraith 2012; see note 40 of ch. 4 above.

10. E.g., Klein 2014. But see Mann 2013, esp. 94–95, who convincingly puts the relation between capitalism and climate change in a much broader and differentiated perspective: "The three great triumphs of the modern period—capitalism, the nation-state, and citizen rights—are responsible for the environmental crisis."

11. Sandel 2012.

12. Examples may be found in Tripp 2006, 150–93, though such totalizing condemnations of capitalism are also not unknown in the West.

Bibliography

Abu-Lughod, J. L. *Before European Hegemony: The World System A.D. 1250–1350*. New York, 1989.

Akerlof, G. A., and R. J. Shiller. *Animal Spirits*. Princeton, 2009.

Albert, M. *Capitalism Against Capitalism*. London, 1993.

Allen, R. C. *The British Industrial Revolution in Global Perspective*. Cambridge, 2009.

Amable, B. *The Diversity of Modern Capitalism*. Oxford, 2003.

Anderson G. *Cityboy: Beer and Loathing in the Square Mile*. London, 2008.

Appleby, J. *The Relentless Revolution: A History of Capitalism*. New York, 2010.

Arnold, D., and J. R. Bongiovi. "Precarious, Informalizing and Flexible Work." *American Behavioral Scientist* 57 (2013): 289–308.

Arrighi, G. *Adam Smith in Beijing: Lineages of the Twenty-First Century*. London, 2007.

———. *The Long Twentieth Century: Money, Power and the Origins of Our Time*. London, 1994.

Ashton, T.S. "The Treatment of Capitalism by Historians." In F. A. Hayek, ed. *Capitalism and the Historians*, 30–61. Chicago, 1963.

Ashtor, E. "Banking Instruments between the Muslim East and the Christian West." *Journal of European Economic History* 1 (1972): 553–73.

Aston, T. H., and C. H. E. Philpin, eds. *The Brenner Debate: Agrarian Class Structure and Economic Development in Pre-Industrial Europe*. Cambridge, 1985.

Atack, J., and L. Neal, eds. *The Origins and Development of Financial Markets and Institutions: From the Seventeenth Century to the Present*. Oxford, 2009.

Atkinson, A. B., et al. "Top Incomes in the Long Run of History." In A. B. Atkinson and T. Piketty, eds., *Incomes: A Global Perspective*, 664–759. Oxford, 2010.

Baptist, E. E. *The Half Has Never Been Told: Slavery and the Making of American Capitalism*. New York, 2014.

Baran, P. A., and P. M. Sweezy. *Monopoly Capital: An Essay on the American Economic and Social Order*. New York, 1966.

Becker, G. S., and G. N. Becker. *The Economics of Life: From Baseball to Affirmative Action to Immigration, How Real-World Issues Affect Our Everyday Life*. New York, 1997.

Becker, U. "Measuring Change of Capitalist Varieties: Reflections on Method, Illustrations from the BRICs," *New Political Economy* 18 (2013): 503–32.

Beckert, S. *Empire of Cotton: A Global History*. New York, 2014.

Bell, D. *The Cultural Contradictions of Capitalism*. New York, 1979.

Berend, I. T. *An Economic History of Nineteenth-Century Europe*. Cambridge, 2013a.

———. *Europe in Crisis. Bolt from the Blue?* New York, 2013b.

Berend, I. T., and R. Schubert. *Markt und Wirtschaft: Ökonomische Ordnungen und wirtschaftliche Entwicklung in Europa seit dem 18. Jahrhundert*. Göttingen, 2007.

Berger, S., and R. P. Dore. *National Diversity and Global Capitalism*. Ithaca, NY, 1996.

Bergheim, S. *Die glückliche Variante des Kapitalismus*. Frankfurt/Main, 2007.

Berghoff, H. "Rationalität und Irrationalität auf Finanzmärkten." In G. Budde, ed. *Kapitalismus: Historische Annäherungen*, 73–96. Göttingen, 2011.

Berle, A., and G. Means. *The Modern Corporation and Private Property*. New York, 1932.

Bernstein, W. J. *A Splendid Exchange: How Trade Shaped the World*. New York, 2008.

Bin Wong, R., and J.-L. Rosenthal. *Before and Beyond Divergence: The Politics of Economic Change in China and Europe*. Cambridge, MA, 2011.

Blackford, M. G. *The Rise of Modern Business: Great Britain, the US, Germany, Japan and China*. Chapel Hill, NC, 2008.

Blanc, L. *Organisation du travail*. 9th ed. Paris, 1850.

Blickle, P. *Unruhen in der ständischen Gesellschaft 1300–1800*. Munich, 1988.

Boltanski, L., and E. Chiapello. *Le nouvel esprit du capitalisme*. Paris, 1999.

Bourne, H. R. Fox. *The Romance of Trade*. London, 1871.

Brantlinger, Patrick. *Fictions of State: Culture and Credit in Britain, 1694–1994*. Ithaca, NY, 1996.

Braudel, F. *Civilization and Capitalism, 15th–18th Century*. Vol 1: *The Structures of Everyday Life: The Limits of the Possible*; vol. 2: *The Wheels of Commerce*; vol. 3: *The Perspective of the World*. New York, 1981, 1982, 1984.

Breman, J. *Outcast Labour in Asia: Circulation and Informalization of the Workers at the Bottom of the Economy*. Oxford, 2012.

Brenner, R. "The Agrarian Roots of European Capitalism," *Past & Present* 97 (1982): 16–113.

———. "Property and Progress: Where Adam Smith Went Wrong." In C. Wickham, ed., *Marxist History-writing for the Twenty-first Century*, 49–109. Oxford, 2007.

Brenner, R. P. "The Low Countries in the Transition to Capitalism," *Journal of Agrarian Change* 1, no. 2 (2001): 169–241.

Brick, H. *Transcending Capitalism: Visions of a New Society in Modern American Thought*. Ithaca, NY, 2006.

Broadberry, S., and B. Gupta. "The Early Modern Great Divergence." *The Economic History Review* 59 (2006): 2–31.

Bücher, K. "Gewerbe." In *Handwörterbuch der Staatswissenschaften*. 4th ed. Vol. 4, 966–99. Jena, 1927.

Buchheim, C. *Industrielle Revolutionen: Langfristige Wirtschaftsentwicklung in Großbritannien, Europa und in Übersee*. Munich, 1994.

Budde, G., ed. *Kapitalismus: Historische Annäherungen*. Göttingen, 2011.

Burnham, J. *The Managerial Revolution*. New York, 1941.

Carruthers, G., and W. N. Espeland. "Accounting for Rationality: Double-Entry Bookkeeping and the Rhetoric of Economic Rationality." *American Journal of Sociology* 971 (1991): 31–69.

Castel, R. *La montée des incertitudes: Travail, protections, statut de l'individu*. Paris, 2009.

Chandler, A. D. Jr. *Scale and Scope: The Dynamics of Industrial Capitalism*. Cambridge, MA, 1990.

―――. *The Visible Hand: The Managerial Revolution in American Business*. Cambridge, MA, 1977.

Chandrasekhar, C. P. "From Dirigisme to Neoliberalism: Aspects of the Political Economy of the Transition in India." *Development and Society* 39:1 (2010): 29–59.

Chaudhuri, K. N. *Trade and Civilization in the Indian Ocean: An Economic History from the Rise of Islam to 1750*. Cambridge, 2005.

Christian, D. *Maps of Time: An Introduction to Big History*. Berkeley, CA, 2004.

Cipolla, C. M. "The Industrial Revolution." In C M. Cipolla, ed., *The Industrial Revolution*, vol. 3 of the Fontana Economic History of Europe, 7–21. London, 1973.

Clark, G. "The Condition of the Working Class in England, 1209–2004," *Journal of Political Economy* 113 (2005): 1307–40.

Cooper, F. "Afrika in der kapitalistischen Welt." In S. Randeria and A. Eckert, eds., *Vom Imperialismus zum Empire*, 37–73. Frankfurt, 2009.

Cooper F., "Capitalism and Capitalists." In P.T. Zeleza, ed., *Encyclopedia of Twentieth-Century African History*, 64–67. London, 2003.

Cowling, K., and P. R. Tomlinson. "Monopoly Capitalism." In D. C. Mueller, ed., *The Oxford Handbook of Capitalism*, 299–327. Oxford, 2012.

Crouch, C. *Industrial Relations and European State Tradition*. Oxford, 1993.

―――. *The Strange Non-Death of Neo-liberalism*. Hoboken, 2011.

Cunningham, W. *The Progress of Capitalism in England*. Cambridge 1916.

Dahrendorf, R. "After the Crisis: Back to the Protestant Ethics? Six Critical Observations." *Max Weber Studies* 10, no. 1 (2010): 11–21.

De Roover, R. *The Rise and Decline of the Medici Bank: 1397–1494*. New York, 1963.

Deutsche Bundesbank. *Deutsches Geld- und Bankwesen in Zahlen 1876–1975*. Frankfurt, 1976.

De Vries, J. *The Industrious Revolution: Consumer Behaviour and the Household Economy 1650 to Present*. Cambridge 2008.

De Vries, J., and A. van der Woude. *The First Modern Economy: Success, Failure and Perseverance of the Dutch Economy, 1500–1815*. Cambridge: 1997.

Dore, R. *Stock Market Capitalism, Welfare Capitalism: Japan and Germany versus the Anglo-Saxons.* Oxford, 2000.

Dunn, R. *The Adventures of Ibn Battuta: A Muslim Traveller of the 14th Century.* Berkeley, CA, 2012.

Duplessis, R. S. *Transitions to Capitalism in Early Modern Europe.* Cambridge, 1997.

Ehmer, J. "History of Work." In *International Encyclopedia of the Social & Behavioral Sciences.* Vol. 24, 16569–75. London, 2001.

Ehrenberg, R. *Das Zeitalter der Fugger: Geldkapital und Kreditverkehr im 16. Jahrhundert.* Vol. 1. Jena, 1896.

Eisenberg, C. "Embedding Markets in Temporal Structures," *Historical Social Research* 36, no. 3 (2011): 55–78.

———. *The Rise of Market Society in England, 1066–1800.* New York, 2014.

Ferguson, M. *The House of Rothschild: The World's Banker 1849–1899.* New York, 1999.

Fernandez-Kelly, P., and J. Shefner, eds. *Out of the Shadows: Political Action and the Informal Economy in Latin America.* University Park, PA, 2006.

Findlay, R., and K. H. O'Rourke. *Power and Plenty: Trade, War, and the World Economy in the Second Millennium.* Princeton, NJ, 2007.

Finley, M. I. *The Ancient Economy.* Berkeley, CA, 1973.

Folsom, B. W., and F. McDonald. *The Myth of the Robber Barons: A New Look at the Rise of Big Business in America.* 6th ed. Hemden, VA, 2010.

Frentrop, P. *A History of Corporate Governance 1602–2002.* Amsterdam, 2002.

Frieden, J. A. *Global Capitalism: Its Fall and Rise in the Twentieth Century.* New York, 2007.

Friedman, M. *Capitalism and Freedom.* Chicago, 1962.

Fulcher, J. *Capitalism: A Very Short Introduction.* Oxford, 2004 (new ed. 2015).

Galbraith, J. K. *Inequality and Instability: A Study of the World Economy Just Before the Great Crisis.* Oxford, 2012.

Ghosh, P. *A Historian Reads Max Weber: Essays on the Protestant Ethic.* Wiesbaden, 2008.

Graeber, D. *Debt: The First 5000 Years.* New York, 2011.

Grassby, R. *The Idea of Capitalism Before the Industrial Revolution*. Lanham, MD, 1999.

Hacker, L. M. "The Anticapitalist Bias of American Historians." In F. A. Hayek, ed., *Capitalism and the Historians*, 62–90. Chicago, 1963.

Hall, K. R. *Maritime Trade and State Development in Early Southeast Asia*. Cambridge, 1984.

Hall, P. A., and D. Soskice, eds. *Varieties of Capitalism: The Institutional Foundations of Comparative Advantage*. Oxford, 2001.

Harris, Robert. *The Fear Index*. New York, 2012.

Hart, K. "Informal Income Opportunities and Urban Employment in Ghana." *Journal of Modern African Studies* 11 (1973): 61–89.

Hartwell, R. M. "The Origins of Capitalism." In S. Pejovich, ed., *Philosophical and Economic Foundations of Capitalism*, 11–23. Lexington, MA, 1983.

Harvey, D. *Kleine Geschichte des Neoliberalismus*. Zurich, 2007.

Haskell, L. "Capitalism and the Origins of the Humanitarian Sensibility." In T. Bender, ed., *The Antislavery Debate: Capitalism and Abolitionism as a Problem in Historical Interpretation*, 107–60. Berkeley, CA, 1992.

Hayek, F. A., ed. *Capitalism and the Historians*. Chicago, 1963.

Heck, G. W. *Charlemagne, Muhammad and the Arab Roots of Capitalism*. Berlin, 2006.

Herbert, Ulrich. *Geschichte Deutschlands im 20. Jahrhundert*. Munich, 2014.

Heynen, R. *Zur Entstehung des Kapitalismus in Venedig*. Stuttgart and Berlin, 1905.

Hilferding, R. *Das Finanzkapital*. Vienna, 1910. Glashütten, Germany, 1977.

Hilger, M.-E. " 'Kapital, Kapitalist, Kapitalismus.' " In O. Brunner et al., eds., *Geschichtliche Grundbegriffe*. Vol. 3, 339–454. Stuttgart, 1982.

Hilton, R., ed. *The Transition from Feudalism to Capitalism*. London, 1976.

Hirschman, A. O. *Rival Views of Market Society and Other Recent Essays*. Cambridge, MA, 1992.

Hobsbawm, E. J., *Industry and Empire: An Economic History of Britain since 1750*. New York, 1999 (repr. of 1968 ed., London).

Hobson, J. A. *The Evolution of Modern Capitalism*. London, 1894.

Honegger, C., et al., eds. *Strukturierte Verantwortungslosigkeit: Berichte aus der Bankenwelt.* Frankfurt, 2010.

Höpner, M. "Sozialdemokratie, Gewerkschaften und Organisierter Kapitalismus, 1880–2002." MPIfG (Max Planck Institut für Gesellschaftsforschung). Discussion Paper 04/10. Cologne, 2004.

Howell, M. C. *Commerce Before Capitalism in Europe, 1300–1600.* Cambridge, 2010.

Hung, H., "Labor Politics under Three Stages of Chinese Capitalism," in *South Atlantic Quarterly* 112 (2013): 203–12.

Ingham, G. *Capitalism.* New York, 2011 (rev. ed. 2013).

Inikori, J. E. *Africans and the Industrial Revolution in England.* Cambridge, 2002.

Inkster, I. *The Japanese Industrial Economy.* London, 2001.

James, H. *Family Capitalism: Wendels, Haniels, Falcks and the Continental European Model.* Cambridge, MA, 2006.

———. "Finance Capitalism." Unpublished manuscript, 2013. To appear in J. Kocka and M. van der Linden, eds. *Capitalism. The Reemergence of a Historical Concept.* London, forthcoming.

Johnson, W. *River of Dark Dreams: Slavery and Empire in the Cotton Kingdom.* Cambridge, MA, 2013.

Jones, E. *Notes to the People.* London, 1851.

Jongman, W. M. "Re-constructing the Roman Economy." In Neal and Williamson, *Cambridge History of Capitalism.* Vol. 1, 75–100.

Jursa, M. "Babylonia in the First Millennium BCE—Economic Growth in Times of Empire." In Neal and Williamson, *Cambridge History of Capitalism.* Vol. 1, 24–42.

Kalleberg, A. L. "Precarious Work, Insecure Workers. Employment Relations in Transition." *American Sociological Review* 74 (2009): 1–22.

Kershaw, I. " 'Working towards the Führer': Reflections on the Nature of the Hitler Dictatorship (1993)." In I. Kershaw, ed. *Hitler, the Germans, and the Final Solution,* 29–48. New Haven, 2008.

Keynes, J. M. *The End of Laissez-Faire.* London 1927.

———. *The General Theory of Employment Interest and Money.* New York, 1936.

Kindleberger, C. P. " 'The Great Transformation' by K. Polanyi," *Daedalus* 103, no. 1 (1974): 45–52.

Kindleberger, C. P., and R. Aliber. *Manias, Panics and Crashes: A History of Financial Crises.* 5th ed. Hoboken, NJ, 2005.

Kirshner, J. *Appeasing Bankers: Financial Caution on the Road to War.* Princeton, NJ, 2007.

Kisch, H. *From Domestic Manufacture to Industrial Revolution: The Case of the Rhineland Textile Districts.* Oxford, 1989.

Klein, N. *This Changes Everything. Capitalism vs. the Climate.* New York, 2014.

Kocka, J. *Arbeitsverhältnisse und Arbeiterexistenzen: Grundlagen der Klassenbildung im 19. Jahrhundert.* Bonn, 1990.

———. "Capitalism: The History of the Concept." In *International Encyclopedia of the Social & Behavioral Sciences.* 2nd ed. vol. 3, 105–110. Amsterdam, 2015.

———. "Entrepreneurs and Managers In German Industrialization." In P. Mathias and M. Postan, eds., *The Cambridge Economic History of Europe.* Vol. 7, pt. 1, 492–589. Cambridge, 1978.

———. "Familie, Unternehmer und Kapitalismus: An Beispielen aus der frühen deutschen Industrialisierung." *Zeitschrift für Unternehmensgeschichte* 24 (1979): 99–135.

———. "Legitimitätsprobleme und–strategien der Unternehmer und Manager im 19. und 20. Jahrhundert." In H. Pohl and W. Treue, eds., *Legitimation des Managements im Wandel,* 7–21. Wiesbaden, 1983.

———. "Reviving Labor History on a Global Scale." *International Labor and Working-Class History* 82 (2012): 92–98.

———. "Siemens und der aufhaltsame Aufstieg der AEG." *Tradition* 17 (1972): 125–42.

———. "Writing the History of Capitalism. *Bulletin of the German Historical Institute* 47 (Fall 2010): 7–24.

Kocka, J., and C. Offe, eds. *Geschichte und Zukunft der Arbeit.* Frankfurt/Main, 2000.

Kocka , J., and M. van der Linden, eds. *Capitalism: The Reemergence of a Historical Concept.* London, forthcoming.

Kornai, J. *The Socialist System: The Political Economy of Communism.* Princeton, NJ, 1992.

Kriedte, P. *Peasants, Landlords and Merchant Capitalists: Europe and the World Economy 1500–1800.* Cambridge, 1983.

Kriedte, P., et al. *Industrialization before Industrialization: Rural Industry in the Genesis of Capitalism.* Cambridge, 1981.

Krippner, G. R. *Capitalizing on Crisis: The Political Origins of the Rise of Finance*. Cambridge, 2011.

Kulischer, J. *Allgemeine Wirtschaftsgeschichte des Mittelalters und der Neuzeit*. 2 vols. 3rd ed. Vienna, 1965.

Kwon, O. Yul. *The Korean Economy in Transition*. Cheltenham, 2010.

Landes, D. S. *The Wealth and Poverty of Nations: Why Some Are So Rich and Some So Poor*. New York, 1998.

Lash, S., and J. Urry. *The End of Organized Capitalism*. London, 1987.

Le Goff, J. *La bourse et la vie: Economie et religion au Moyen Age*. Paris, 1986.

———. *Le Moyen Age et l'argent*. Paris, 2010.

———. *Marchands et banquiers au Moyen Age*. Paris, 1956.

Lee, Ching Kwan *Against the Law: Labour Protests in China's Rustbelt and Sunbelt*, Berkeley 2007.

Lenin, V. I. *Imperialism: The Highest Stage of Capitalism*. Moscow, 1920.

Li, B. "Was There a Fourteenth-Century Turning Point?" In P. J. Smith and R. van Glahn, eds., *The Song-Yuan-Ming Transition in Chinese History*. Cambridge, MA, 2004.

Lichtenstein, N., ed. *American Capitalism: Social Thought and Political Economy in the Twentieth Century*. Philadelphia, 2006.

Lis, K., and H. Soly. *Worthy Efforts: Attitudes to Work and Workers in Pre-Industrial Europe*. Leiden, 2012.

Lu, H. "Arrested Development: Cotton and Cotton Markets in Shanghai, 1350–1843." *Modern China* 18 (1992): 468–99.

Lucassen, J., ed. *Global Labour History*. Bern, 2006.

Luxemburg, R. *The Accumulation of Capital*, trans. by Agnes Schwarzschild. New York 1968.

Mackey, J. *Conscious Capitalism: Liberating the Heroic Spirit of Business*, Cambridge, MA, 2013.

Maier, A. *Der Heuschrecken-Faktor: Finanzinvestoren in Deutschland*. Munich, 2007.

Maier, Ch. S. "Capitalism and Territory." In G. Budde, ed., *Kapitalismus: Historische Annäherungen*, 147–63. Göttingen, 2011.

Maiti, D., and K. Sen. "The Informal Sector in India: A Means of Exploitation or Accumulation?" *Journal of South Asian Development* 5 (2010): 1–13.

Mann, M. "The End May Be Nigh, But for Whom?" In I. Wallerstein et al., *Does Capitalism Have A Future?*, 71–97. Oxford, 2013.

———. *The Sources of Social Power*. Vols. 1–4. Cambridge, 1993–2013.

Marks, S. G. "The Word 'Capitalism': The Soviet Union's Gift to America." *Society* 49 (2012): 155–63.

Marx, K., and F. Engels *Werke* (abbrev. in notes: *MEW*). Vols. 1–45. Berlin, 1956–1990.

McCraw, T. K. *Profit of Innovation: Joseph Schumpeter and Creative Destruction.* Cambridge, MA, 2007.

Medick, H. *Weben und Überleben in Leichingen 1650–1900: Lokalgeschichte als Allgemeine Geschichte.* Göttingen, 1996.

Mendels, F. "Proto-Industrialization: The First Phase of the Industrialization Process." *Journal of Economic History* 32 (1972): 241–61.

Merrill, M. "The Anticapitalist Origins of the United States." *Review. The Journal of the Fernand Braudel Center.* 13:4 (1990): 465–97.

———. "How Capitalism Got Its Name," *Dissent*, Fall 2014, 77–81.

———. "Putting 'Capitalism' in Its Place: A Review of Recent Literature." *William and Mary Quarterly*, 3rd ser., 52 (1995): 315–26.

Middleton, J. *The World of the Swahili: An African Mercantile Civilization.* New Haven, CT, 2009.

Mielants, E. H. *The Origins of Capitalism and the "Rise of the West."* Philadelphia, 2007.

Mihm, S., and N. Roubini. *Crisis Economics: A Crash Course in the Future of Finance.* New York, 2010.

Milanovic, B. "A Short History of Global Inequality: The Past Two Centuries." *Explorations in Economic History* 48 (2011): 494–506.

Mirowski, P., and D. Plehwe, eds. *The Road from Mont Pèlerin: The Making of the Neoliberal Thought Collective.* Cambridge, MA, 2009.

Muller, Jerry Z. *Capitalism and the Jews.* Princeton, NJ, 2010.

———. *The Mind and the Market: Capitalism in Western Thought.* New York, 2002; paperback 2003.

Myant, M., and J. Drahokoupil. *Transition Economics: Political Economy in Russia, Eastern Europe, and Central Asia.* London, 2010.

Naughton, B. *The Chinese Economy: Transitions and Growth.* Cambridge, MA, 2007.

Neal, L., and J. G. Williamson, eds. *The Cambridge History of Capitalism.* 2 vols. Cambridge, 2014.

North, M. *Geschichte der Ostsee: Handel und Kulturen.* Munich, 2011.

O'Brien, P. "European Economic Development: The Contribution of the Periphery." *Economic History Review* 35, no. 1 (1982): 1–18.

———. "Ten Years of Debate on the Origins of the Great Divergence." *Reviews in History*. file://localhost/(http//:www.history.ac.uk:reviews). 30 November 2010.

Offe, C. *Disorganized Capitalism: Contemporary Transformation of Work and Politics*. London, 1985.

Ogilvie, S. *Institutions and European Trade: Merchant Guilds 1000–1800*. Cambridge, 2011.

Ogilvie, S., and M. Zerman, eds. *European Proto-Industrialization*. Cambridge, 1996.

Osterhammel, J. *The Transformation of the World: A Global History of the Nineteenth Century*. Princeton, NJ, 2014.

Osterhammel, J., and N. P. Petersson. *Globalization: A Short History*. Princeton, NJ, 2009.

Parthasarathi, P. "Was There Capitalism in Early Modern India?" In R. Datta, ed., *Rethinking a Millennium: Essays for Harbans Mukhia*, 342–60. Delhi, 2008.

Passow, R. *"Kapitalismus."* 2nd ed. Jena, 1927.

Persson, K. G. "Markets and Coercion in Medieval Europe." In Neal and Williamson, *Cambridge History of Capitalism*. Vol. 1, 225–66.

Piketty, T. *Capital in the Twenty-First Century*. Cambridge, MA, 2014.

Pirenne, H. "The stages in the history of capitalism," *American Historical Review* 19 (1914): 494–515.

Plumpe, W. *Wirtschaftskrisen: Geschichte und Gegenwart*. Munich, 2010.

Polanyi, K. *The Great Transformation*. New York, 1944.

Pomeranz, K. *The Great Divergence: China, Europe and the Making of the Modern World Economy*. Princeton, NJ, 2000.

Proudhon, P.-J. *Idée générale de la révolution au dix-neuvième siècle*. Paris, 1851.

Pryor, F. L. *Capitalism Reassessed*. Cambridge, 2010.

Ptak, R. *Die chinesische maritime Expansion im 14. und 15. Jahrhundert*. Bamberg, 1992.

Redlich, F. *Der Unternehmer*. Göttingen, 1964.

Reinhard, W. *Geschichte der Europäischen Expansion*. Vol. 2. Stuttgart, 1985.

———. *Kleine Geschichte des Kolonialismus*. 2nd ed. Stuttgart, 2008.

Reinhard, W., et al., *Empires and Encounters: 1350–1750*. History of the World. Cambridge, MA, 2015.

Rendall C. "An Asian Route to Capitalism," *American Sociological Review* 62 (1997): 843–65.

Rifkin, J. *The Zero Marginal Cost Society: The Internet of Things, the Collaborative Comments, and the Eclipse of Capitalism.* Palgrave, 2014.

Rodinson, M. *Islam and Capitalism.* London, 2007.

Rösener, W. *Die Bauern in der europäischen Geschichte.* Munich, 1993.

Rothschild, E. *Economic Sentiments: Adam Smith, Condorcet and the Enlightenment.* Cambridge, MA, 2001.

Roy, T. "Capitalism in India in the Very Long Run." In Neal and Williamson, *Cambridge History of Capitalism.* Vol. 1, 165–92.

Sabean, D. "German International Families in the Nineteenth Century." In C. H. Johnson et al., eds., *Transregional and Transnational Families in Europe and Beyond*, 229–52. New York, 2011.

Safley, T., ed. *The History of Bankruptcy: Economic, Social and Cultural Implications in Early Modern Europe.* New York, 2013.

Salvioli, G. *Le capitalisme dans le monde antique.* Paris 1906.

Salvucci, R. "Capitalism and Dependency in Latin America." In Neal and Williamson, *Cambridge History of Capitalism.* Vol. 1, 403–30.

Sandel, M. J. *What Money Can't Buy: The Moral Limits of Markets.* New York, 2012.

Sanyal, K. *Rethinking Capitalist Development: Primitive Accumulation, Governmentality and Post-Colonial Capitalism.* London, 2007.

Schäffle, A. E. F. *Kapitalismus und Sozialismus mit besonderer Rücksicht auf Geschäfts- und Vermögensformen.* Tübingen, 1870.

Schama, S. *The Embarrassment of Riches: An Interpretation of Dutch Culture in the Golden Age.* New York, 1987.

Schilling, H. *Martin Luther: Rebell in einer Zeit des Umbruchs.* Munich, 2012.

Schluchter, W. *Die Entzauberung der Welt: Sechs Studien zu Max Weber.* Tübingen, 2009.

———. *Rationalism, Religion, and Domination: A Weberian Perspective*, trans. by Neil Solomon. Berkeley, CA, 1989.

Schmid, G., and P. Protsch. "Wandel der Erwerbsformen in Deutschland und Europa." Discussion paper SPI 2009–505. Berlin (WZB), 2009.

Schulz, K. *Handwerk, Zünfte und Gewerbe: Mittelalter und Renaissance.* Darmstadt, 2010.

Schumpeter, J. A. *Business Cycles: A Theoretical, Historical and Statistical Analysis of the Capitalist Process*. Vol. 1. New York, 1939.

———. *Capitalism, Socialism, and Democracy*. 2nd. ed. New York, 1947.

———. *The Theory of Economic Development*, trans. by Redvers Opie. Oxford, 1961.

Sée, H. *Les origines du capitalisme moderne*. Paris 1926.

Segre, S. "A Comment on a Recent Work by Heinz Steinert on Max Weber." *Österreichische Zeitschrift für Geschichtswissenschaften* 23 (2012): 16–32.

Sennett, R. *The Corrosion of Character*. New York, 1998.

Shadwell, A. "Capitalism." *Edinburgh Review* 232 (July 1920): 69–83; 233 (January and April 1921): 80–99, 371–86.

Shatzmiller, M. "Economic Performance and Economic Growth in the Early Islamic World, 700–1000." *Journal of the Economic and Social History of the Orient* 54 (2011): 132–84.

Shonfield, A. *Modern Capitalism: The Changing Balance of Public and Private Power*. Oxford, 1965.

Sinn, H.-W. *Kasino-Kapitalismus*. Berlin, 2009.

Sklansky, J. "The Elusive Sovereign: New Intellectual and Social Histories of Capitalism." *Modern Intellectual History* 9 (2012): 233–48.

———. "Labor, Money and the Financial Turn in the History of Capitalism." *Labor: Studies in Working Class History of the Americas* 11 (2014): 23–46.

Sokoll, T. *Europäischer Bergbau im Übergang zur Neuzeit*. Idstein, Germany, 1994.

Sombart, W. *Der moderne Kapitalismus*. 2 vols. Leipzig, 1902 (3 vols. 2nd ed. Munich and Leipzig 1924–1927).

Soros, G. *The Crisis of Global Capitalism*. New York, 1998.

Spree, R., ed. *Konjunkturen und Krisen in der Neueren Geschichte* 2011.

Spuler, B. *Iran in frühislamischer Zeit*. Wiesbaden, 1952.

Standing, G. "Economic Insecurity and Global Casualization. Threat or Promise?" *Social Indicators Research* 88 (2008): 15–30.

Stanziani, A. *Bondage: Labor and Rights in Eurasia from the Sixteenth to the Early Twentieth Centuries*. New York, 2013.

Stark, W. "Techniken und Organisationsformen des Hansischen Handels im Spätmittelalter." In S. Jenks and M. North, eds., *Der Hansische Sonderweg?*, 101–201. Cologne, 1993.

Stearns, P. N. *The Industrial Revolution in World History*. Boulder, CO, 1993.

Steinert, H. *Max Webers unwiderlegbare Fehlkonstruktionen: Die protestantische Ethik und der Geist des Kapitalismus*. Frankfurt, 2010.

Steinfeld, R. J., ed. *Coercion, Contract and Free Labor in the Nineteenth Century*. Cambridge, 2001.

———. *The Invention of Free Labor: The Employment Relation in English and American Law and Culture, 1350–1870*. Chapel Hill, NC, 1991.

Streeck, W. *Buying Time: The Delayed Crisis of Democratic Capitalism*. London, 2014a.

———. "How Will Capitalism End?" *New Left Review* 87 (May/June 2014b): 35–64.

———. *Reforming Capitalism: Institutional Change in the German Political Economy*. Oxford, 2009.

Subrahmanyam, S., ed. *Money and the Market in India 1100–1700*. Oxford, 1994.

Swanson, P. *An Introduction to Capitalism*. London, 2012.

Swedberg, R. *Max Weber and the Idea of Economic Sociology*. Princeton, NJ, 1998.

Tawney, R.H. *Religion and the Rise of Capitalism: A Historical Study*. London 1926.

Teich, M., and R. Porter, eds. *The Industrial Revolution in National Context: Europe and the USA*. Cambridge, 1996.

Temin, P. *The Roman Market Economy*. Princeton, NJ, 2012.

Thomas, K., ed. *The Oxford Book of Work*. Oxford, 1999.

Thompson, E. P. *The Making of the English Working Class*. London, 1963.

———. "The Moral Economy of the English Crowd in the 18th Century." *Past and Present* 50 (1971): 76–136.

Tilly, C. "Demographic Origins of the European Proletariat," in D. Levine, ed., *Proletarianization and Family History*. Orlando 1984, 1–85.

Tilly, C., and C. Tilly. *Work under Capitalism*. Boulder, CO, 1998.

Trentmann, F., ed. *The Oxford Handbook of the History of Consumption*. Oxford, 2012.

Tripp, C. *Islam and the Moral Economy: The Challenge of Capitalism*. Cambridge, 2006.

Troeltsch, W. *Die Calver Zeughandlungscompagnie und ihre Arbeiter: Studien zur Gewerbe- und Sozialgeschichte Altwürttembergs.* Jena, 1897.

Udovitsch, A. L. "Merchants and Amirs: Government and Trade in Eleventh Century Egypt." *Asian and African Studies* 22 (1988): 53–72.

———. *Partnership and Profit in Medieval Islam.* Princeton, NJ, 1970.

Van Bavel, B. "The Medieval Origins of Capitalism in the Netherlands." *Low Countries Historical Review* 125, nos. 2–3 (2010): 45–79.

Van der Linden, M. "Who is the Working Class? Wage Earners and Other Labourers." In M. Atzeni, ed., *Workers and Labour in a Globalized Capitalism: Contemporary Themes in the Theoretical Issues,* 70–84. Houndmills, UK, 2014.

———. *Workers of the World: Essays Toward a Global Labor History.* Leiden, 2008.

Van der Linden, M., and J. Rojahn, eds. *The Formation of Labour Movements 1870–1914.* 2 vols. Leiden, 1990.

Van der Wee, H., and G. Kurgan-van Hentenryk, eds. *A History of European Banking.* 2nd ed. Antwerp, 2000.

Van Zanden, J. L. *The Long Road to the Industrial Revolution: The European Economy in a Global Perspective, 1000–1800.* Leiden, 2009.

———. "Tracing the Beginning of the Kuznets Curve: Western Europe during the Early Modern Period." *Economic History Review* 48 (1995): 643–64.

Van Zanden, J. L., et al. "The Changing Shape of Global Inequality 1820–2000." *Review of Income and Wealth* 60, no. 2 (2014a), 279–97.

———, eds. *How Was Life? Global Well-Being Since 1820.* Paris, 2014b.

Veblen, T. *The Instinct of Workmanship and the State of Industrial Arts.* New York, 1914.

Vogl, J. *Das Gespenst des Kapitals.* 2nd ed. Zurich, 2010–2011.

Vosco, L. F. et al., eds. *Gender and the Contours of Precarious Employment.* New York, 2009.

Vries, P. *Escaping Poverty: The Origins of Modern Economic Growth.* Göttingen, 2013.

———. "Europe and the Rest: Braudel on Capitalism." In G. Garner and M. Middell, eds., *Aufbruch in die Weltwirtschaft: Braudel wiedergelesen,* 81–144. Leipzig, 2012.

Wallerstein, I. *The Modern World-System.* Vols. 1–3 (New York, 1974, 1980, 1989); vol 4 (Berkeley, CA, 2011).

Wallerstein, I., et al. *Does Capitalism Have A Future?* Oxford, 2013.

Weber, M. *Economy and Society: An Outline of Interpretive Sociology,* ed. by Guenther Roth and Claus Wittich. Berkeley, CA, 1978 (repr. 2013).

Weber, M. *General Economic History,* trans. by Frank H. Knight. Glencoe, IL, 1927 (repr. 1950).

———. *The Protestant Ethic and the Spirit of Capitalism.* 1920. Rev. ed., trans. and intro. by Stephen Kalberg. New York, 2010.

Weber, M. *Zur Sozial- und Wirtschaftsgeschichte des Altertums. Schriften und Reden 1893–1908.* Max Weber Gesamtausgabe. Vol. 6, sect. 1. Tübingen, 2006.

Williams, R. *Keywords: A Vocabulary of Culture and Society.* New York, 1976.

Windolf, P., ed. *Finanzmarkt-Kapitalismus: Analysen zum Wandel von Produktionsregimen.* Wiesbaden, 2005.

Winkler, H. A., ed. *Organisierter Kapitalismus: Voraussetzungen und Anfänge.* Göttingen, 1974.

Wolfe, T. *Bonfire of the Vanities.* New York, 1987.

Wood, E. M. *The Origin of Capitalism: A Longer View.* London, 2002.

Zakim, M., and G. J. Kornblith, eds. *Capitalism Takes Command: The Second Transformation of 19th Century America.* Chicago, 2012.

Zeuske, M., ed. *Handbuch Geschichte der Sklaverei: Eine Globalgeschichte von den Anfängen bis heute.* Berlin, 2013.

Index of Names